BAR HOPPING

THRU AMERICA

BAR HOPPING

THRU AMERICA

Taverns, Bars, Saloons and Night Clubs -
An American History

Terry W. Lyons

ISBN: 978-0-9827442-4-6

Cover Design by Tyler Hollis

Cover Photo by Jen Ryder

Published by Fiction Publishing, Inc.
5626 Travelers Way
Fort Pierce, FL 34982

Printed in the United States of America

CONTENTS

INTRODUCTION

The American drinking establishment, called a tavern in its early days, a saloon in its heyday, and everything from a gin mill to a nightclub in between, has been a cornerstone of this country from the very beginning.

Uniquely, its fundamental purpose has never changed. It has always served as a gathering place where individuals can seek and, sometimes, find comfort. This may be in the form of entertainment, information, or companionship. Sometimes it has served as a place to get out of the cold, or as a floor to sleep on. In its early days the tavern was everything: post office, courtroom, bank, employment agency - you name it!

Today the bar is a place to view sports on TV with friends, play pool or darts, dance, view strippers, or listen to a comedian or a piano player. But the "good old neighborhood bar" still performs the basic function of offering comfort.

A wonderful description of a neighborhood bar is given in the opening paragraph of J.R. Moehringer's 2005 edition of "The Tender Bar: A Memoir."

Quote: "We went there for everything we needed. We went there when thirsty, of course, and when hungry and when dead tired. We went there when happy to celebrate, and when sad to sulk. We went there after weddings and funerals, for something to settle our nerves, and always for a shot of courage before. We went there when we didn't know what we needed, hoping someone might tell us. We went there when looking for love, or sex, or trouble, or for someone who had gone missing, because sooner or later everyone turned up there. Most of all we went there when we needed to be found."

The bar in this country has been in existence for over 300 years. There aren't many businesses with a record like that!

1

During those 300-plus years it has changed, of course, and it keeps changing. It helped unite the colonies, settle the West, provide tax revenue for the Civil War, and serve as a refuge for millions and millions of immigrants from Europe. It was forced to go underground during Prohibition, and managed to flourish and establish a culture all its own.

The bar in America continues under siege in the 21st century as health concerns regarding smoking and drinking, drinking and driving, and higher and higher alcohol taxes and prices, all threaten its survival. But it marches on with $18 martinis, 50-inch TV sets, micro-brew beers, and the undying need of the individual for "comfort."

THE BEGINNING

The wine urges me on, the bewitching wine, which sets even a wise man to singing and to laughing gently and rouses him up to dance and brings forth words which were better unspoken. Homer (800-700 BC), The Odyssey

Drinking alcoholic beverages can be traced back in history to the ancient Greeks in 6000 B.C. Signs for "public houses" go back 2,000 years to Pompeii and Herculaneum when a board showing two slaves carrying a wine skin noted the shop of a wine merchant. In the ancient city of Pompeii you can see the remains of wine shops, and massive stone bars and benches for the customers.

In ancient Rome wine leaves symbolized Bacchus, the God of Wine, and were displayed outside wine outlets called tabernae, from which the term tavern is derived. Chequers was a popular game in Pompeii taverns; and the Romans brought it to England.

The fermentation process of breaking sugar down into alcohol occurs naturally when fruits are exposed to air. Mead is an ancient drink made from the fermentation of honey and water. Wine is a fermented drink made from grapes and, of course, is frequently mentioned in the Bible.

The ancient Egyptians were major cultivators of grapes for wine making; and popular festivals were always celebrated with drinking wine. Archeologists have developed theories that indicate the Egyptians even imported wine from the areas known today as Turkey and Iran. These wines were labeled for intended use, i.e., festival wine, wine for paying taxes, and wine for "offerings." The tombs of the Pharaohs contain wine cellars filled with jars of wine.

In Ireland, historians trace ale brewing using wild barley to over 800 years ago. The ruins of the Saint Francis Abbey, from the period, can still be seen on the grounds of Smithwick's brewery in Kilkenny, Ireland.

Monasteries preserved the art of winemaking through the Middle Ages. They introduced the cork, which permitted them to age wine in bottles. The Church had a virtual monopoly on the growing of grapes and the production of both wine and spirits. Taverns and cabarets became the centers of social and intellectual life in European medieval cities.

The Dutch drank huge quantities of alcohol, mainly beer, and drinking accompanied all social settings, religious or secular, business or pleasure. In 1613, Amsterdam had 518 licensed alehouses, a ratio of one for every 200 men, women and children.

In England, at this time, alehouses were more numerous than any other public place. These were managed mainly by women, hence the term "alewives."

Both the Dutch and the English had many laws on the books to regulate the sale and consumption of alcohol in the early 17th century. These laws, rules, regulations and customs were all brought to America by the early settlers, and helped shape the drinking patterns of this country.

Beer arrived in America on the Mayflower when the Pilgrims landed at Plymouth Rock in 1620. One theory holds that the Pilgrims were blown off course, originally planning to land farther south; but since they were almost out of beer they were forced to land at Plymouth. Beer had been brewed at the Roanoke Colony of Sir Walter Raleigh in 1587.

Europeans had a very poor opinion of water; and they regarded alcohol as not only safer, but essential to good health. Water, it was believed, was better suited for barnyard animals than for humans. Alcohol was not just a substitute for water; it was considered a food necessary for good health. It was credited with many medicinal attributes including being able to cure colds, fevers, snakebites, and even broken bones. In addition, alcohol was a welcome supplement to monotonous diets. A favorite quote of the time: "Water, it's good for navigation."

17th CENTURY

"He who has not been at a Tavern knows not what paradise is."
— Henry Wadsworth Longfellow

Taverns have been a part of America since the founding of the colonies in the early 1600s. Villages had only two public buildings, the church or meetinghouse, and the tavern; usually they were located side by side. This is contrary to our present laws forbidding taverns near houses of worship. Sometimes the tavern doubled as the meetinghouse and vice versa. The tavern was a welcome respite from the cold, unheated meeting house; taverns were warm and cozy. The first tavern was opened in Boston in 1634 by Samuel Cole.

The tavern served many purposes in early America; just as it did 200 years later when the West was settled. Taverns were not just a place to drink and gather together socially; the tavern was also used for town meetings, entertainment, jury trials, centers for gossip, exchanging ideas, and eventually it became the first post office in town.

Copying the English, laws were passed demanding that taverns provide food and lodging for travelers, including their horses. In 1656, the General Court of Massachusetts made towns liable to a fine for not "providing and sustaining" an "ordinary" for travelers. It should be noted that various terms were applied to the early taverns. These included: tavern, ordinary, public house (i.e., pub) and inn; these terms were not always interchangeable. The name tavern was usually used in New England and New York State; Pennsylvania used the term inn; in the South they were called ordinaries. Another rarely used term in colonial days was "racon" tavern, meaning that although a private residence, travelers might be accommodated; and upon leaving they paid a reasonable reckoning.

One unusual practice of American taverns that differed from their European counterparts was the custom of bed sharing.

5

Strangers, men, women and children were all expected to share the beds available. Anyone who objected to this was considered obnoxious. Europeans were appalled at this practice, which continued well into the 18th century. The reason behind this custom was very simply the shortage of available space as the nation grew rapidly.

It was not unusual for the tavern owner to ascend the stairs in the middle of the night and add another guest to the group already sharing the accommodations. The guest simply crawled into bed wherever a space appeared available. Bed partners were not separated by male/female—all slept together. Occasionally some rules did apply; "no more than five to a bed, no boots to be worn in bed."

Only the most respected citizens were chosen to run the taverns and bars in early America. This was an important job with many ordinances to enforce. In any village or town the controlling members considered the inn must be a safe and hospitable place for travelers, women and, of course, themselves. Because taverns played such an important role in local affairs, the upper classes believed that they should be well regulated, orderly, and respectable. Rules were established for the selection of those eligible to hold a tavern license. For example: only voters, church members, deacons, and ministers might be eligible. This made the license holders beholden to the town selectmen, council, or other governing group.

In the 1600s a New England innkeeper was selected with great care and was a man of importance. He was often the best known, most popular, and most picturesque person in town. He was a man of character and often held public office; or he might be the town magistrate, member of the legislature, or a commander in the local militia.

The innkeeper had many duties in addition to providing food, drink, and lodging. One of his most important responsibilities was enforcement and observation of the many rules and regulations covering taverns. Europe once again was the source for the various rules governing drinking. Attempts to control the alehouse in England had medieval precedence. In fact, laws covering the sale of alcoholic beverages are included in the code of Hammurabi of ancient Babylonia (1750 B.C.). The code provided the death penalty could be applied to a proprietor for diluting drinks. We might have a lot of dead bartenders if this rule were in effect today.

By the late Middle Ages an informal system of licensing had developed in some areas. During the 1500s English Parliament introduced statutory licensing. The purpose of the law was to limit the number of alehouses.

Licensing of taverns in America ruled from the very beginning. The reasons were many and included limiting the number of establishments, selecting the proprietor, and raising money for the government. Licenses varied and some were for "beer and wine only," or "only out-of-doors," or "hard drinks only," etc. The innkeeper who paid for the license was charged with many obligations: he could not serve drunkards; he could not serve Indians; the prices he could charge were regulated; no games nor entertainment were permitted; and, as mentioned earlier, he had to provide food and lodging for travelers and their horses; no drinking after curfew—9:00 P.M; no drinking before 3:00 P.M. on the Sabbath, unless the person was a boarder at the inn.

As early as 1633 many laws were passed to cover drunkenness and disorderly behavior. The penalties included fines, stocks, whipping, and even wearing a large red "D" set on a white cloth around the neck.

To obtain a tavern license in New Jersey in the late 1600s and the early 1700s, it was necessary for the applicant to "have the recommendation of 10 respectable freeholders, with a standing of good repute for honesty, and for temperance." The tavern must have at least two spare beds, and be provided with "horse room"; and the host might neither "game himself or herself, nor suffer any person to game for money." Prices were fixed by law. "For a good breakfast, 40 cents; good dinner 50 cents; good supper 40 cents, lodging 12 cents." Innkeepers were forbidden to sell drink on the "Lord's Day," except for necessary refreshments. Considerable latitude seems left to the innkeeper as to what was "necessary."

Drinking in early America, just as in England, became a major source of revenue for the colonies. Money was obtained by licensing the tavern, making the innkeeper post a bond to ensure good behavior, placing an excise tax on the alcohol; and finally by fining the drunkards. All this has not changed today, over 350 years later.

THE TAVERN

"Nothing has yet been contrived by man, by which so much happiness is produced as by a good tavern or inn." — *Dr. Samuel Johnson, 18th century British writer.*

A typical early American tavern would be rigidly square. The taproom would be just inside the entrance; adjacent to the bar would be a room with a long table for eating. Upstairs would be the sleeping quarters, one or two rooms with two to four beds. A huge fireplace would occupy the main downstairs room; hooks on either side were available for housing firearms. Tobacco and pipe drawers were nearby and smoking tongs were hung next to the pipe drawer; with these the smoker could lift a coal from the fireplace with which to light his pipe. Sometimes the tavern parlor walls would be painted with a mural or covered with wallpaper showing a forest scene or a fox chase.

The taproom or barroom, if separate, contained another enormous fireplace. It had a sanded floor, seats and chairs, and frequently, a tall, crude desk would occupy a corner of the room. The main feature, of course, was the bar; depending upon the class of the tavern, this could be ornate and elaborate, or quite humble.

As towns began to emerge in the colonies, taverns became more numerous, and were much better establishments. In 1648, one quarter of the buildings in New Amsterdam, (New York City), had been turned into tap houses for the sale of beer, brandy and tobacco. The City Tavern in New Amsterdam (1641-1642), built entirely of stone, was converted in 1653 into the City Hall since it was one of the largest and most prominent buildings on the island of Manhattan. It remained the City Hall until the 1880s!

At the other extreme, almost any building or house could be licensed to dispense alcohol. Many, especially in rural areas, consisted of only one room. This room served as the bar,

9

kitchen, dining room and bedroom. They were often small, dirty, with bad food and poor service.

A good tavern always had liquor, a fireplace, sanded floors, a large parlor or lounge, and a bar on one side with tables and chairs for dining. Separate areas for eating did not become popular until the 1800s.

Picture the barkeeper surrounded by barrels, bottles, tankards, jars of spices and sugar loaves—and, always a hot poker ready to be plunged into a mug of "flip," making a foam collar around the rim of the tankard. There was a great fondness for hot drinks, flips, toddies, and hot buttered rum.

The ordinary alehouse, tavern, or whatever, served a multitude of purposes from the very beginning and, as time went forward into the 1700s, its role grew.

The tavern was a welcome respite from the stark, cold, unheated meetinghouse. Members of the congregation often took "a break" at the tavern for drink and nourishment, and then returned to their services which were extremely long by today's standards - lasting just about all day Sunday. Not like today, when the old joke applies, "He was faster than the last Mass at a summer resort."

The tavern was occupied primarily by men, but often managed and owned by women. The selfish reason for this was often based on the local town council not wishing to financially support women and their children following the death of a husband. It was more prudent to grant a tavern license than to place the widow on the poor roles.

Often the licenses were granted only "to sell liquor out-of-doors." This was because proprietors were responsible for keeping an orderly house, and since in early New England society women were assumed incapable of commanding men; it was felt that their tavern could be the site of great disorders. Women as guests or customers were seldom present in the upper and middle class taverns; but were often present in low-end establishments as patrons or prostitutes.

Taverns in the 17th century, just as today, were

differentiated by the status of patrons and proprietors. Some were allowed to dispense only beer and cider, while the more exclusive ones dispensed wine and brandy.

The low-end establishments were usually clustered near the waterfront, grog shops that catered to mariners. It is important to note that many laws governed the sale of alcoholic beverages to seamen. Laws differentiated between seamen who were contracted to a ship, and those that were currently "at Liberty"; it was against the law to serve the former without permission from the respective shipmaster.

The neighborhood taverns in the cities were visited by the craftsmen and clerks. The more spacious and well-decorated places were reserved for the upper levels of society. Country inns were destined to serve whoever came by.

These taverns were the social center of the town and the activities and functions were many. One of the most important early roles of the tavern, which continues to this day, was recreation.

As the town and village tavern developed the early rules prohibiting games and entertainment began to disappear. In the 1600s, billiards and darts appeared in taverns; and gambling became a major source of recreation. Most gambling in the early years involved cards. Whist, a form of bridge, was a popular game with the upper classes; other early forms of entertainment included bull baiting, cockfighting, chequers and dice.

Upper rooms in taverns were frequently used as jails, and the tavern parlor was the courtroom. It was common practice that both the judge and the jury drank before and during the trial. The only one not drinking was the defendant. Justice was swift, and so was the punishment. Public punishment included stocks, whipping, and hanging. These afforded some of the best entertainment for the tavern crowd.

Known as "Execution Day," a hanging was a grand day for taverns. Ten thousand people witnessed Burnham's hanging in 1805 in New England. Our ancestors found in criminals and all the accompaniments of crime their chief source of diversion. The only excitement and stirring of emotions that occurred in their lives came through the recounting of crimes and offenses, and the public sight of the punishment of these crimes and offenses; and, of course, a public execution was the pinnacle of their excitement. A magazine known as the "Police Gazette" existed well into the 20th century. It satisfied its subscribers with lurid details of crimes on a nationwide basis. The supermarket tabloids on sale today cater to the curiosity and excitement associated with major criminal acts.

A word about food: Taverns, especially rural ones, were required by law to serve food, and variations of this law persist in many states to this day.

Early tavern food, as you may imagine, was not particularly tasty; another reason for the large quantities of alcohol consumed. In summer, fruits and vegetables were plentiful; but winter meals were largely composed of meat.

One of the most inhumane practices consisted of using "turnpit dogs" to roast meat on a spit. The little, patient creatures, long bodied and crooked-legged, spent their lives helping to cook meat they seldom tasted. When meat was to be roasted, the dogs went into a caged wheel, and a burning coal was placed behind them. If they stopped, their rear legs got burned. It was hard work since the piece of meat often weighed twice as much as the dog, and it took at least three hours of roasting.

In early America, corn dominated the American diet. In winter Americans ate dried, parched corn kernels; in summer they preferred roasted green ears, in autumn freshly boiled, golden ripe ears dripping with melted butter. But it was corn pummeled into hominy or ground into meal that was ever present at all meals in all seasons. It appeared on the table three times a day as Johnnycakes, or corn bread, Indian pudding with milk and sugar, or the ever-present corn mush. Corn was also feed for the pigs. Ordinary bread was baked with flour composed of corn and rye; bread made with white wheat flour was a luxury for the rich or for special occasions.

Each day it was calculated the typical adult American

male ate a pound of bread and a pound of meat, usually salt pork. Only on special occasions did the Americans vary from this monotonous diet. Fruit, game birds, oxen and venison were substituted on holidays and celebrations. These meals always included alcohol of some sort—beer, cider, whiskey, or wine —no water.

Many early taverns in the South offered an "ordinary," defined as "a public meal regularly provided at a 'fixed price' in an eating house or tavern." The "ordinary" became so common a feature of American establishments that the term was often used as a synonym for taverns. Establishments generally served the main meal or "ordinary" between the afternoon hours of one and three o'clock (this was known at that time as dinner, not lunch). This was a public meal offered every afternoon and many places offered this meal at no charge. This custom was the predecessor of the popular "free lunch" of the saloon period (1870-1920).

By 1668 so many small ordinaries existed in the colony of Virginia that laws were passed restricting the number in each county to one at the court house, and possibly another at the wharf or ferry. Next, the magistrates tried to limit the drinks sold in these places to beer and cider; and private individuals were warned not to sell any sort of drink or liquor whatsoever. This was impossible to enforce and, before long, everyone had plentiful supplies of Madeira, Canary, Malage and Fayal wines. But these ordinaries did very, little business as lodging places. And, the farther south you went, the scarcer they became.

Taverns in the South were generally known as "ordinaries" until the beginning of the 18th century. In the large towns of Virginia, however, comfortable taverns were established everywhere. In fact, the best taverns in America were located in southern cities beginning with the Fountain Inn in Baltimore and extending to Williamsburg, Virginia and the Raleigh Tavern.

CIDER

"People who don't drink are at a disadvantage; when they wake up that is as good as they're going to feel all day." — W.C. Fields

American drinking in the 1600s consisted primarily of cider and beer, and later rum. Cider drinking was popular in New England where apple orchards were abundant and hard cider was made by fermenting apples. The hard cider was usually 5-7% alcohol and was stored in barrels and drunk year-round.

The colonists, young and old, drank this alcoholic drink on every occasion. Infants in arms drank mulled hard cider at night. Old men began the day with a quart of hard cider before breakfast. At Harvard and Yale, cider was passed in two-quart tankards from hand to hand around the table. The pegs on the inside of early wooden drinking vessels marked the limit for each drinker before he passed the vessel to the next person; hence, the expression "to take someone down a peg or two."

Hard cider accompanied every meal, including breakfast. It was consumed at work, in the fields, and at every social occasion. Cider remained the most common beverage in the colonies until the 19th century. It is interesting to note that because alcohol was considered a food essential to good health; it was consumed by all religions, including the Quakers and the Puritans. The habit of "dramming" was widespread. This was the practice of taking a fortifying glass in the forenoon and again in the afternoon.

Apples were so plentiful in the northeast and in parts of Virginia, Pennsylvania, Ohio and New York, that they were usually free for the picking.

Throughout the Northeast farmers pressed their fruit on wooden frames that stood in nearly every orchard. In contrast with brewing, which required substantial capital, skilled labor, and a local, densely populated market, cider making was so easy,

14

cheap and low skilled, that a farmer could afford to press apples strictly for home use. Cider was not usually marketed because its bulk made its shipment unprofitable; hence, little was drunk in the South or in cities.

Though inexpensive, cider had high alcohol content. To avoid spoilage, it was often fortified with distilled spirits until it contained at least ten percent alcohol, twice that of beer. There were even stronger forms; cider royal, which was hard cider mixed with distilled apple brandy or whiskey; and applejack, which was the 20% alcohol liquor that could be poured off after cider had been set outside to freeze on an autumn night.

During the winter a typical New England family could be expected to consume a barrel a week. Even John Adams, who railed against distilled spirits for half a century, drank a tankard full every single morning of his life. A tankard is equivalent to a quart. John Adams lived to be 90 in an era when most males didn't make it to 50!

In 1840, the Whig Party nominated William Henry Harrison as its presidential candidate, and the campaign symbol was a barrel of cider. The "cider campaign" in which the Whigs offered free cider to all who would vote for Harrison brought him a landslide victory.

Between 1770 and 1792, cider consumption increased 200% to become the most popular drink in America.

While cider was definitely the drink of choice in early America; it was not the only alcoholic drink available. Shortly after 1650, trade with Barbados, in the West Indies, began a development that had a profound effect on colonial drinking patterns.

Molasses from sugar cane provided the raw materials for rum production; and it soon became one of the most popular beverages in the colonies. It was very cheap and could be used to make punch and Flip. Flip was an especially popular wintertime favorite. Flip was made from rum and beer sweetened with sugar and warmed by plunging a red-hot poker into the mug in which it was served. An earthen pitcher or huge pewter mug served as a useful utensil in which to make American Flip. Such a vessel would be filled about two-thirds with strong beer to which would be added molasses, sugar, or diced pumpkin for sweetening, and about a gill of rum for flavor. Four gills equal one pint.

Flip glasses, huge tumblers without handles, were the drinking vessels in which the Flip was often served. Some of them would hold three or four quarts each. Face it: these folks were drinkers on a major scale.

The tavern host usually had the basic recipe for Flip already made. This could be a pint of cream, four eggs and four pounds of sugar. When someone ordered Flip, the bartender would fill a quart mug two-thirds full of bitter beer, add four huge spoonfuls of the above mixture, a gill of rum; and then thrust a red-hot poker into it. This gave it a sweet bitter taste. Imagine an evening spent in a tavern full of people, laughing and drinking, fire roaring, full of life—no TV, no juke box, just each other. Flip glasses are collectors' items today.

Another popular drink was "punch." This drink originated in the English colonies in India. In Hindu, "punch," means five—for the five ingredients: tea, arrack, sugar, lemon, and water. Tea was replaced by rum, and later by numerous other alcoholic beverages.

The British invented a very elegant punch bowl called "*The Monteith,*" named after a man who wore a scalloped coat. The rim of the bowl was scalloped like *Monteith's* coat, and was used for hanging the ladle, wine glasses and the lemon strainer. The rim was separate from the bowl and could easily be removed. Sometimes the bowl alone was passed and drunk from without glasses.

Every sea captain who sailed the West Indies was expected to bring home a turtle, in addition to a barrel of rum, for a feast with his friends. A turtle was deemed an elegant gift; and usually a keg of lime accompanied the turtle. Limejuice was considered the best of all "sourings" for punches. Turtle feasts at taverns were major events.

The other popular drink in America from the very

beginning was beer. Early colonists made their own beer, "small beer," about one percent alcohol—spoiled quickly—made by soaking grain in water; once or twice a week the housewife made this beer at home.

Beer was made from maize as early as 1620 in Virginia. William Penn brewed and sold beer in Bucks County, Pennsylvania in 1644; he also owned a tavern.

Beer continued to be popular with the early colonists, especially the Dutch. The early Dutch colonists were primarily beer drinkers, and did not partake of cider, wine and rum like the others.

The Dutch West India Co. established a brewery in New Amsterdam as one of its first enterprises. The company also imported wines and brandy in quantity; and to bolster business they urged residents to sell company products from their homes.

The beer was made primarily from hops and barley and mostly home brewed until the German immigration around 1840.

Beer - some recipes:
1. Beer for the family:
    A handful of hops to a pail-full of water, a half-pint of molasses. Boil two-three hours, add molasses while hot, strain and when lukewarm, add yeast. When the froth subsides the beer is ready.

2. Common Beer:
    Two gallons of water to a large handful of hops is the rule. Adding a fresh-gathered spruce or sweet fern makes the beer more agreeable. Boil for 2-3 hours, strain, add a teacup of molasses per gallon. Stand till lukewarm, add good yeast, and shake well together. Beer will be fit to drink the next day.

Wine was another alcoholic drink consumed in significant quantities, and the term "sack" was applied to a broad variety of dry white wines—not just sherry. Wine's popularity, as with rum, resulted from it being very cheap. The favorite flavoring for mulled wine was nutmeg, which was scarce and expensive.

In the 17th and 18th centuries, drinking in taverns may have accounted for no more than one quarter of the alcoholic beverages consumed. To not have alcoholic beverages available in your home was considered a major breach of hospitality. America was only 5% urban as late as 1820; however, in the urban areas, taverns flourished.

COLONIAL DAYS

"If God had intended for man to drink water, he would not have made him with an elbow capable of raising a wine glass." — Ben Franklin

As America entered the 18th century, the number and the quality of taverns increased rapidly. By 1721, Philadelphia had 94 licensed establishments, or one for every 54 people in the city; New York had a ratio of one for every 91 residents, and Boston had a ratio of one per 94 residents.

For comparison, in the 1700s Dublin, Ireland had a population of 25,000; and there were 2,000 alehouses, 300 taverns, and 1200 brandy shops. It was estimated that about one-third of the houses in the city sold alcoholic beverages. Today, Dublin, with a population of over one million has 1,000 pubs. The Irish government has been on a program to reduce pubs since the 1920s. By the way, the oldest pub in Ireland is Grace Neil's Inn at Donaghadee, built in 1611—not too long before drinking places began appearing in America.

In America, as cities and towns grew in population, and the government expanded its role; the licensing of taverns became increasingly strict. This, of course, expanded the number of illegal establishments. Licensing continued to serve dual purposes: controlling drinking and raising money. Although licensing was designed to limit the number of establishments, the ratio of taverns to population remained fairly constant during the 1700s.

About the beginning of the 18th century, a change occurred in popular drinking patterns. Distillation methods allowed the French to make brandy from wine. The Russians and Swedes made clear alcohol from potatoes and spoiled grain. The Scots and Irish made whiskies from grain; and the West Indies used sugar cane to make rum. As the supply of distilled spirits, especially rum, increased, the price dropped and they became the drink of choice throughout the colonies, replacing beer and ale.

The officials noticed an increase in alcohol abuse; drunkenness and disorderly conduct accompanied the use of hard liquor. The individual colonies passed extensive laws attempting to define drunkenness and appropriate punishment. These were difficult to enforce. They also went to extreme lengths to limit drinking on the Sabbath. Tavern keepers were responsible for not permitting drunkenness on their premises. Some colonies passed laws establishing time limits for visiting a tavern—usually one hour maximum.

These laws, governing both the individual's behavior and the behavior of the tavern keeper, were generally enforced in the New England colonies; but rarely applied in the rural south.

The typical pattern of growth in places like Philadelphia, Boston, and New York City was based on dense clusters of bars near the waterfront. The harbor acted as a magnet for taverns because this was where commercial business was done. They, of course, also attracted the mariners who were eagerly seeking booze, companions and entertainment.

As the cities grew, the taverns followed the population growth inland. Taverns in the city improved immensely; many of the better ones were located in the South.

Tavern density in Charleston, South Carolina remained steady during the years preceding the Revolution. In 1762 there were 64 fully licensed taverns, 10 of which included a permit to have a billiard table. Including licenses for selling drinks out-of-doors, it is estimated that 1 in 13 of all the dwellings in Charleston was licensed to sell liquor. This does not include an unsubstantiated number of illegal outlets operating in the city.

Some of the city taverns were quite grand places and the term "ordinary" was replaced by the term "tavern." Many splendid homes eventually became taverns. In Philadelphia, Benjamin Franklin's home became a tavern; so did the Bingham mansion built in 1790 by the richest man of his day.

The taverns in restored Williamsburg, Virginia offer wonderful examples of the finest places of the time. The Raleigh

Tavern on Duke of Gloucester Street was erected about 1717 and became the center for social and political life before the Revolution. George Washington, Thomas Jefferson, and Patrick Henry are a few of the Patriots who helped make history in this tavern. It was in the Apollo Room that students at the College of William and Mary are said to have founded the Phi Beta Kappa Society in 1776. The building was reconstructed after a fire in 1859.

The Raleigh's role is typical of a tavern in colonial America. It served as a center for social, commercial, and political gatherings, small, private, and large public dinners, lectures, exhibits, and auctions of merchandise, property, and the enslaved.

During "Publik Times," when the courts were in session, the Raleigh hummed with activity. Gentlemen and ladies attended elegant balls in the popular Apollo Room. Sturdy tavern tables held dice boxes and cards, and pipe smoke filled the air. Good fellowship and business deals were sealed by a toast of Madeira wine or a pewter tankard of ale. A huge celebration was held at the Raleigh after the Treaty of Paris ended the Revolution.

Like many taverns of the period, the Raleigh was a large-scale enterprise. Outbuildings provided a kitchen with a huge fireplace, bakery, stable for horses, and accommodations for slaves.

Wetherburn's Tavern on the south side of Duke of Gloucester Street near the capital, figured prominently in the commercial life of Williamsburg, and has been in continuous use for over 200 years. George Washington was a frequent visitor. The outbuildings include the customary kitchen, smokehouse, well house and dairy.

Chowning's Tavern in Williamsburg has an area just inside the front door with vertical bars similar to a jail cell. These bars, known as a "portcullis gate," similar to the gate on a castle drawbridge separated the bartender from the customers. Hence, the term "bar" became another word for drinking establishments.

The food served in these taverns was good and was, of

21

course, seasonal. Chowning's Tavern attracted the "ordinary sort," and served food similar to an 18th century ale house: Brunswick stew, pulled pork barbecue, and cider cake.

Christiana Campbell's Tavern was a favorite of George Washington where he often enjoyed the oysters. The King's Arms Tavern opened in 1772, and became one of Williamsburg's more "genteel" establishments. They dined on peanut soup, grilled meats, fowl and fish. Dessert might include a cherry truffle, a colonial favorite.

Shields Tavern, one of the very early taverns in Williamsburg, attracted a lower gentry, and successful, middling customers. The fare here consisted of food available from nearby farms and rivers; and included barnyard chicken roasted on a spit, cornbread, stuffed quail with wild boar sausage, and syllabub (a dessert-style drink).

The City Tavern of Philadelphia was an elaborate establishment—a two-story brick building measuring 50 feet by 46 feet, made even more fashionable because it was set back a considerable distance from the street. Patrons ascended a stately flight of stone steps to the first floor, which contained the bar and public rooms, each extending the entire length of the building. On the second floor were two clubrooms that could be altered to be one large space nearly fifty feet in length. The second floor also contained a long gaming room.

The Indian King Tavern, a converted Philadelphia mansion, consisted of 18 rooms, 14 with fireplaces, and stables for up to a hundred horses. These were definitely upper-class establishments for the wealthy citizens. Thomas Jefferson drafted the Declaration of Independence at the Indian Queen Tavern in Philadelphia.

Taverns for lower and middleclass patrons varied enormously. People often converted their own houses into pubs or ordinaries merely by posting a sign, serving liquor, and setting up additional beds for guests. If the place had only one room, then all activities occurred in the same space—drinking, eating, entertaining, and sleeping.

Dancing was popular in New England in the period between strict Puritan days and the Revolution, which accounts for the many ballrooms in these old taverns. An old account of a wedding dance given in New London, Connecticut states that it stopped "at 45 minutes past midnight," but before that there had been "92 jigs, 52 contrivances, 45 minuets, and 17 hornpipes" danced by the guests.

The list of activities, celebrations and special occasions occurring at these taverns in the 1700s is almost endless, and varied with the location, class, size, patronage, etc.

One of the largest celebrations was an occasion for the ordination of a new minister, "Ordination Day." The event was observed in the meeting house and celebrated in the tavern. Often an especially good beer was brewed called "ordination beer," and an "ordination ball" was held at the tavern. Guests attended from miles around, and most were lodged at the local tavern.

As discussed, the tavern keeper was obligated by law to provide food and lodging for patrons and their horses. In addition, the tavern was the source of newspapers, mail, gossip, advertising, messages, and entertainment. Slaves and servants were advertised and sold at taverns from Boston to Charleston. Goods, including ships of commerce, were sold at taverns. Lectures took place and courses, such as geometry, were taught; and traveling artisans plied their trades in the taverns of the cities. The tavern was the focal point of all social activities in a town. The taverns of Boston were the original business exchanges; they combined counting house, Exchange office, reading rooms, and the bank.

The list goes on and on. Plays were presented in taverns, meetings of various organizations met in the taverns; i.e., the Freemasons, book clubs met in taverns, fox hunting, turkey shoots and bull and bear baiting also took place.

The fact that the local militia met on the Village Green for weekly drills, and always adjourned to the tavern, led to many accidental shooting incidents—the predecessor of "drinking and driving" problems.

GAMING

"The trouble with jogging is that the ice falls out of your glass."
– Martin Mull

Sports of all sorts were played in the taverns of early America. Again, most of these were imported from England; but some were homegrown; and most survived and are played in bars today.

Large taverns in urban areas had multiple rooms so patrons could choose to play cards, billiards, backgammon—or nothing. Most of these games, and sports, involved men and losses from gambling at billiards became such a problem that billiard tables were outlawed in the city of Philadelphia in 1744. To avoid this rule many patrons simply journeyed out of town, where tables were easily available.

Whisk, similar to bridge, was a popular card game for the upper classes since some training was required. "All-Fours" was the card game favored by the lower classes; and winning depended more on luck than on skill. Dice was another popular tavern game and a box with dice was usually available at the bar.

Special sporting events were always held near a tavern; and drinking and gambling were the major ingredients. In the South, cockfights were prevalent, and were advertised in the local paper. Horse racing was popular in the colonies; and the day usually began and ended at the local pub. Purses for the winning horse were often substantial, but side betting was the major sport. The Jockey Club of Philadelphia was organized in 1766 by "seventy-one gentlemen of the turf," and race meetings were held once a year.

"Bull and bear baiting" was a particularly gruesome diversion practiced in the rural areas in the 18th century. This involved chaining the bear or bull to a post and unleashing a pack of dogs as the challenge.

Drinking contests were a part of tavern life in early

America; and there are many records of deaths reported from these gambling challenges. "In 1736, Thomas Apty, a Philadelphia plasterer, found his way to the Red Lion on Elbow Lane. He wagered he could drink a gallon of hard cider in an hour and a half. He accomplished the feat and dropped dead on the spot." Roger Addams, an inebriated patron in a Dorchester County, Maryland tavern bet he could drink all the wine left in a decanter in one draught. He won the wager and died a few minutes later. This dangerous "game" persists till this day, especially on college campuses. Drinking "shots" is one especially dangerous and popular custom today. Not a year goes by without reports of multiple deaths on college campuses resulting from fraternity hazing, initiation rites, drinking challenges, etc.—all involving drinking excessive amounts of alcohol. One of the newer fads on college campuses is called "loading up" or "front loading" or "pre-gaming." The idea is for 18-, 19- and 20-year-olds to get drunk before going out because they have to be 21 once they get to a bar.

CLUBS

"He who drinks fast, pays slow." – Benjamin Franklin

Clubs were an integral part of the tavern scene in early America and remain popular to this day. It was a natural urge for men of similar interests to bond together for a variety of reasons but the major reason was usually an excuse for drinking. The tavern owners encouraged clubs because they guaranteed a regular clientele; and the proprietors usually offered them some sort of perks; i.e., discounted drinks, free food, and, of course, a free place to meet on a cold, winter evening.

Gentlemen, who by reason of their wealth, prestige and popularity set the tone for society, belonged to drinking clubs that met privately in the back rooms of taverns. These retreats, modeled after the London clubs immortalized by Samuel Johnson, flourished in cities such as Boston, New York, and Annapolis.

Some of these clubs met every night of the week, but most met weekly, and many included supper. They would talk, smoke, sing, laugh, debate, argue—and drink. Membership was usually restricted by status. The drinking at these gatherings often consisted of passing a bowl of punch. In the upper class clubs the members usually consumed at least a bottle of wine each at a single meeting.

These clubs were noteworthy for the population segments that were always excluded: women, blacks, slaves, and people of lower ranking.

Benjamin Franklin founded a club in Philadelphia during his beginning years as a printer. He called it the Junto. Membership included Franklin and three young men who worked for the same printer. They first met at an alehouse, and from time to time members were added or departed; but the total always remained about a dozen. As Franklin described it, they were there to enjoy a chat, a laugh, a drink, and a song; but at every meeting a member presented a paper; and earnest discussions took place between drinks.

Franklin was only 21 when he started the club and it lasted for forty years, meeting on Friday nights. It might have lasted longer if Franklin had not left for a lengthy time of public service in 1754. It was a couple of fellow Junto Club members that financed Franklin in his original printing business. Franklin belonged to other clubs in Philadelphia like the Masons, and the Club of Honest Whigs in London.

Philadelphia was fond of clubs, and there was no shortage of applicants wanting to join Franklin's Junto Club. When this happened, instead of enlarging the Club, Franklin arranged for members to start new clubs on the Junto model. Franklin used the Junto Club, not only as a means to advance his own interests, but also as a way to improve life in Philadelphia. One of his first ventures was to encourage members to bring books to the Friday meetings so they could have access to each other's volumes. The number of books available did not satisfy Franklin; and he then persuaded fifty people to fund a library where all subscribers could borrow. The result was the Library Company of Philadelphia, still flourishing today.

He also used the Junto and its affiliated clubs to promote a new club for fighting fires. Several volunteer fire fighting clubs were formed and fire damage in Philadelphia was drastically reduced. And, as we all know, volunteer fire-fighting organizations play a significant role in America today. It is not at all unusual for the volunteer firehouse in suburban or rural America to include some sort of clubroom facilities for drinking, eating, and recreation. The Junto Club also established the academy that later became the University of Pennsylvania.

REVOLUTIONARY WAR YEARS

"Good wine is a necessity of life." – Thomas Jefferson

As America entered the 1760s and relations with England began to deteriorate, it's important to consider the major role played by the tavern.

In the 1760s, Philadelphia had about 150 licensed "drink sellers," or 1 per 105 citizens. Other proportions: Boston-135, 1 per 123 citizens; New York City-287, 1 per 55 citizens; Charleston, South Carolina-101, 1 per 96 citizens.

As discussed, the tavern was the center of social life, the meeting place, and the place to discuss and debate the news. It naturally became the place to begin planting the seeds to revolt against the rules, laws and taxes being passed by the British Parliament to control the colonies. There was probably not a single tavern that did not play a part, large or small, in the Revolutionary War.

Daniel Webster called the tavern "the headquarters of the Revolution"; others said it was "A Cradle of Independence." Rebellion was plotted in hundreds of taverns throughout the thirteen colonies.

As the war progressed, the role of the tavern increased. The British, the merchant seamen, and the Revolutionaries used taverns as jails, hospitals, barracks, ammo depots, officer headquarters, courtrooms, places for secret meetings and as recruiting stations.

In 1765, The Sons of Liberty* was formed through meetings at taverns. They drank and toasted and schemed within the walls of the Province Arms Tavern in New York City. Concerts and duels alternated with suppers and society-meetings; dancing committees and the governors of Kings College poured in and out of the Province Arms. The Province Arms had opened in New York City in 1754 in a residence built around 1700, and considered a mansion at the time. The laying of the cornerstone for Kings College was celebrated with a huge party at the Province Arms. In 1792 it was sold and torn down; and the City Hotel was built in its place.

In Massachusetts, the Westborough Minute Men made the Gale tavern their rendezvous when the Revolution broke out, and there the captain trained his company. At the "Powder Alarm," the men were ready and before daybreak 72 of them left the tavern and marched down the old trail to meet the British at Concord. Even the aged landlord would not be left behind, but shouldered his musket and went along.

It was at the Green Dragon tavern in Boston that men fortified themselves before dressing as Indians and embarking on the Boston Tea Party. Paul Revere and 30 compatriots used the Green Dragon Tavern as an intelligence headquarters for information about the movements of British soldiers and Tories. The Green Dragon became a hospital during the war.

-

*The Sons of Liberty was a secret organization formed in the American colonies to protest the Stamp Act and other rulings of the British government. In 1765 the Sons of Liberty in Boston would meet secretly at the base of a large elm tree at the corner of Washington and Essex streets whenever the red flag floated from a pole fastened to the highest branch. Following these secret meetings the participants would adjourn to the nearby tavern. The Sons of Liberty and the Liberty Pole concept spread to all thirteen colonies prior to the Revolutionary War.

Before the Battle of Lexington the men met at John Buckman's alehouse for a round of drinks. It was at Winchester's Black Horse Tavern where the soldiers re-assembled after the Battle of Lexington. During the siege of Boston in 1775, The St. George Tavern was an advance post of the Continental Army. The British attempted to destroy it many times, and finally set it on fire on July 31, 1775.

In 1700, in New York City, Colonel Cortland gave the lot, on which Fraunces Tavern still stands, to his son-in-law, Etienne DeLancy, a French Huguenot. Mr. DeLancy built a house on the lot for himself and his wife, Anne, in 1719.

In 1737, a ball was given by dancing-master Henry Holt, in the house formerly owned by the DeLancys who had moved in 1730. For many years afterwards, balls, concerts, and other shows were held at the house.

In 1762, the property was bought for 2,000 pounds by Samuel Fraunces, a man of French extraction, who came to America from the West Indies, and had operated a tavern in New York for the previous seven years. He opened the newly purchased house as a tavern in 1763, calling it the Queen's Head, and it has been open as a tavern ever since. The "Long Room" in the tavern became famous in American History and in the stormy days before the Revolution many meetings of protest were held there.

In 1775 the tavern was offered for sale. The advertisement read, "The Queen's Head Tavern near the Exchange is three and one-half stories high with tile and lead roof, has 14 fireplaces, almost excellent large kitchen, five dry cellars, etc." The sale was unsuccessful and Fraunces decided to run it himself, and continued doing so all through the Revolution. Fraunces rendered such aid to the American cause, including aid to prisoners, that after the war, Congress gave him a vote of thanks and a gratuity of 200 pounds, a considerable sum at the time.

In 1783, the house was first called Fraunces Tavern and, although it had other names afterward, this one has persisted. Many stirring and interesting happenings have occurred in

Fraunces Tavern and its Long Room. Here the Sons of Liberty and the Vigilance Committee met in 1774 and arranged to attack the ship London, docked at the East India Company Wharf, where they broke open her cargo of tea chests, emptying the contents into the water of the bay, thus celebrating New York's own tea party.

Merchants met at Fraunces Tavern to consider uniting with the other colonies in calling a congress. In the same year, 1774, the Massachusetts delegates to this Continental Congress were entertained in the Long Room at a banquet given them by the New York delegates. It was in the Long Room that, in 1783, Washington bade his memorable farewell to his officers. Long Room window sash weights were appropriated in 1776 for use in cannon balls at Fort Montgomery and Fort Clinton in New York City.

Fraunces Tavern was reconstructed exactly as the original in 1907, and is Manhattan's oldest building, and is still on its original site. Antiques from the Revolutionary War era furnish the tavern, and the architecture is one of New York's few remaining examples of restored Early Georgian architecture. Located at the corner of Broad and Pearl streets in Manhattan, Fraunces Tavern is definitely worth a visit. There is an operating bar and restaurant on the first floor and a museum occupies the second and third floors.

The importance of alcoholic drinks at the time of the Revolution is demonstrated in a letter from General George Washington to the President of Congress dated August 16, 1777. In the letter Washington laments the scarcity of spirits and suggests, "I would beg leave to suggest the propriety of erecting Public Distilleries in different states. The benefits arising from the moderate use of strong liquor have been experienced in all armies, and are not to be disputed."

(In contrast, 80 years later in the Civil War, temperance representatives called on Abraham Lincoln at the White House and blamed the defeats of the Union troops on intemperance among the soldiers.)

The following is a brief list and description of a few taverns that played a part in the Revolution.

The Wayside Inn in Sudbury, Massachusetts dates back to 1716. Thanks to industrialist Henry Ford who preserved the site in 1923, today it is a national historical site with10 guest rooms and a dining room that is open to the public daily. Lt. Colonel Ezekiel Howe hosted fellow revolutionaries here to drink ale and discuss politics. Howe led a contingent to Concord on April 19, 1775 when the War began.

In typical fashion the barroom is on the left as you enter with a low ceiling, exposed beams, fireplace, and a small bar in the corner.

On the right is a parlor. It was in this parlor in October 1862 that Henry Wadsworth Longfellow visited with friends. A year later, using this locale, Longfellow published a collection of poems, "The Tales of a Wayside Inn." These tales became classics of American literature, and include the famous "Listen my children and you shall hear of the midnight ride of Paul Revere."

The Munroe Tavern built in 1695 continued as a tavern until 1858. After the battle of Concord, the British brought their wounded into the tavern. General Washington dined in the upstairs bedroom in 1789, having arrived in his own coach with two secretaries and six servants. The Munroe Tavern historical site is located at 1332 Massachusetts Avenue in Lexington, Massachusetts.

George Washington and his staff assembled and had dinner at McCorkey's Ferry Inn on December 25, 1776 prior to crossing the Delaware and surprising the Hessians in the Battle of Trenton. The list continues.

Golden Plough Tavern, York, Pennsylvania. A typical frontier tavern of half timber and brick built in the 1740s. It was in the nearby Gates House that the Marquis de Lafayette prevented the overthrow of General George Washington as head of the Continental Army at the famous Conway Cabal meeting.

Michie Tavern, Charlottesville, Virginia. The oldest

portion dates from 1740. In 1746 Patrick Henry's father sold the tavern to John Michie. The family operated this tavern until 1910 and entertained guests including Jefferson, Madison, Monroe and Lafayette. Many furnishings are original.

Tandee's Tavern, Savannah, Georgia. Here Rebels raised The Liberty Pole and convened The Provincial Congress in the summer of 1775.

Catamount Tavern, Bennington, Vermont. It was here that Ethan Allen met with the local Council of Safety and the Green Mountain Boys to plan their skirmishes with the British authorities between 1770 and 1774, and then the capture of Ft. Ticonderoga in 1775. It was called The Green Mountain Tavern in those days, and around the time of the Civil War it became the Catamount Tavern. It was destroyed by fire in 1871.

Rising Sun Tavern, Fredericksburg, Virginia. Like all colonial taverns, the Rising Sun Tavern was a focus of pre-war political activity. The owner was from Hamburg, Germany. Gerhard von der Wieden rose to brigadier general in the Revolution and was known to his troops as "Joe Gourd." Washington and Lafayette celebrated here after the victory of Yorktown.

Gadsby's Tavern, Alexandria, Virginia. Built in 1752 at 132 Royal Street. Known as City Tavern. George Washington used the tavern frequently as a military headquarters in battles against the French and Indians prior to the Revolution. In November of 1799 he reviewed the local militia from the tavern steps, ending his military career where it had started 45 years earlier. A gigantic reception was held here for Lafayette in 1824.

Spread Eagle Tavern, Berwyn, Pennsylvania. Harry "Lighthorse" Lee took refuge in this tavern with seven companions and fought off a British force on January 20, 1778. This was the beginning of Lee's exceptional career in the Revolution. He was the father of Civil War Confederate general, Robert E. Lee.

Greene Inn, Buckingham, Pennsylvania. Known during the Revolution as Bogart's Tavern, this was headquarters for

General Nathaniel Greene in December 1776 before the famous crossing of the Delaware, and the attack on Trenton. After this, it was renamed the Greene Inn. It is open to the public.

White Horse Tavern, Newport, Rhode Island. America's oldest tavern, built 1673. Restored.

Wrights Tavern, Concord, Massachusetts. Here militia assembled on April 19, 1775, when the courthouse bell sounded the alarm and British officers arrived to establish their command post and take refreshments.

Stonewall and Wooded Tun Tavern, Philadelphia. The U.S. Marine Corps was founded here in 1775. The Tun Tavern was built in 1685 and named "Tun" for an Old English word for a container of beer, "tun." When the Continental Congress enacted a decision to form the continental Marines, known today as the U.S. Marine Corp, recruitment was based at the tavern, and the proprietor, Robert Mullen, was made "Chief Marine Recruiter." The tavern burned in 1781.

WHISKEY REBELLION OF 1794

"Bacchus hath drowned more men than Neptune." – Dr. Thomas Fuller

The taxes on alcoholic beverages had their beginning with the establishment of the new government in 1789. Alexander Hamilton was appointed Secretary of the Treasury and was responsible for proposing taxes to finance the new government.

Large amounts of revenue were needed to pay the war debts, and it was obvious that taxes beyond import duties would be needed. Hamilton favored a tax on "domestic spirituous liquors." He knew, just as today, that it would be difficult for politicians to oppose a tax that promised to raise money and reduce drunkenness at the same time.

As an added incentive to New Englanders, a tax on whiskey would maintain price parity with rum; which had already been hit with an import duty because it was either imported, or distilled from imported molasses.

Hamilton's whiskey tax was not a success. Protests in the South and West arose immediately and tax collectors were having a difficult time collecting the tax.

The Whiskey Rebellion of 1794 was the first serious threat to the authority of the new Federal Government. The first excise tax, the 1791 tax on whiskey, had created an uproar among the farmers of western Pennsylvania where the economy of the upper Monongahela Valley was virtually based on distilled spirits.

Since farmers raised more grain than they could eat or ship, they found it necessary to convert the excess into a product that was easy to transport—rye whiskey. The whiskey was practically an alternate currency in the region, and was readily exchanged for money. The Federal tax ranged from 7 cents to 25 cents a gallon between 1791 and 1795.

A Federal Militia was organized and over 15,000 troops, more than Washington commanded at times during the Revolution, marched from Trenton, Philadelphia and Baltimore for six weeks to reach Western Pennsylvania. The show of strength easily put down the insurrections, which had been terrorizing the area, even threatening to attack Pittsburgh. The challenge had been met—men of one state would invade the territory of another to protect the authority of the Federal Government.

The hated tax was repealed in 1802 under Thomas Jefferson's presidency. With the abolition of the tax, the price of whiskey fell, consumption rose; and whiskey came to be used as rum had once been, as a form of currency.

The end of the whiskey tax signaled a change in the drinking habits of this country. The availability of cheap spirits enabled every man to be "drunk as a lord" the prestige of drunkenness declined. Heavy drinking was no longer a sign of wealth and status. As an unintended consequence, the elite, upper class began to adopt a new habit of sobriety. The upheavals of the Revolution had enabled the masses to take control of the taverns.

Amid these social changes began an undercurrent of thinking that alcohol was not the good, God-given substance bestowed on mankind to heal all sorts of ills and solve life's problems. The seeds for a quarrel about the benefits vs. the problems of alcohol had been planted. This quarrel continues into the 21st century.

As early as 1772, Dr. Benjamin Rush, a physician living in Philadelphia, educated at Edinburgh College of Medicine in Scotland, had begun questioning the effects of too much alcohol. Rush served as the Continental Army's Surgeon General during the Revolutionary War, and his observations strengthened his convictions concerning the harmful effects of drinking strong spirits. He especially condemned the Army's rum ration, asserting that it caused numerous diseases including fevers and fluxes.

As substitutes, Rush recommended various mixtures of milk, buttermilk, cider, small beer, molasses, vinegar and water. Dr. Rush's first pamphlet urging moderate drinking, eating, and exercise appeared in 1772. This was followed in 1782 by a newspaper article he authored, titled "Against Spirituous Liquors".

In 1784, Dr. Rush wrote "An Inquiry into the Effects of Ardent Spirits on the Human Mind." Dr. Rush, by now a signer of the Declaration of Independence, was the most prominent physician in America at this time.

This paper was contrary to the long held opinion that alcohol was not only good for you, but it was necessary for you to perform in a productive manner. Rush at this time had no quarrel with alcohol in beer or wine, only with "ardent spirits." Rush felt that drunkenness was the major deterrent to the success of the new republic. He was the first to associate alcohol with addiction. His idea was to switch people from rum and whiskey to the "more healthful beer and wine." Rush was eventually known as "The Father of Temperance."

This was the beginning of the many temperance movements in this country. The cause was initially taken up by the Presbyterians, and later by the Methodists.

The 1784 pamphlet was a very skillful presentation of scientific evidence, logic, and argument, and it received a very sympathetic and vigorous response. Influential people agreed with Dr. Rush, and soon his findings were receiving widespread publication.

One of his primary supporters was Jeremy Belknap, a Boston minister, and later President of Harvard College. Through Belknap, Rush began to enlist the support of the clergy in his anti-alcohol campaign.

Rush published a "Moral and Physician's Thermometer" that correlated beverages with various physical conditions. Water, milk and small beer brought health, wealth, and happiness. Drinks made from mixing alcohol resulted in sickness, idleness and debt. Straight whiskey and rum caused crime, chronic disease and punishment, and incessant drinking resulted in death. Prohibition arrived about 140 years later.

Drinking in the late 1700s in America actually increased. Americans continued to drink universally and in tremendous quantities. At the time of the Revolution, the yearly consumption of alcohol was estimated to be three and one-half gallons of 200 proof, pure alcohol per person. Since the mid-19th century, consumption per capita has never exceeded two gallons per person, per year. "Proof" is a measure of alcohol content commonly used in the U.S. (100 percent alcohol equals 200 proof.) In the 18th century American whiskey trade, farmers mixed gun powder with whiskey and lit it. If it flashed, it was the proper "proof"—mainly alcohol instead of water.

The Founding Fathers were major drinkers. James Madison had a pint of whiskey every morning to start his day. George Washington was a heavy consumer of alcohol. Washington was typical of the upper class in Virginia, and it is reliably reported that he regularly drank from a half pint to a pint of Madeira wine, in addition to punch and beer.

Patrick Henry tended bar in his father-in-law's taproom at Hannon Court House, Virginia and as noted earlier, John Adams began each day with a quart of hard cider.

When you consider the normal practice was to drink at every meal, and in between, the level of competence of these founding fathers was amazing. The Continental Army received a daily whiskey ration of four ounces—a gill.

George Washington, following his retirement from the presidency and moving to Mount Vernon in 1797, built a distillery where he processed his neighbors' surplus grain.

Washington erected a 2,250 square foot distillery making it the largest in early America. In 1799 Washington produced 11,000 gallons of whiskey, worth the then-substantial sum of $7,500.

A letter from George Washington to his nephew, Colonel William A. Washington in 1799 states:

"Two hundred gallons of whiskey will be ready this day

for your call, and the sooner it is taken the better, as the demand for this article in these parts is brisk."

The distillery ceased operating in 1814 when the building burned. Excavation and reconstruction began in 2000 with a grant from the distilled spirits industry. The operating distillery is now open to the public from April to November.

A 50-milliliter bottle (a mini) of a limited-edition blend of 11 America whiskeys vatted and bottled at the distillery is available in the gift shop for $25 including a shot glass.

The museum serves as a gateway to the American Whiskey Trail, which takes in historic sites and museums in five states.

Here is a list of the National Historical sites on the tour:

1. Fraunces Tavern, New York City. This has been described earlier.
2. Gadsby's Tavern Museum, Alexandria, Virginia. Founded in 1792 as the City Tavern and Hotel. This place was frequented by George Washington, Thomas Jefferson, John Adams and other prominent gentlemen of the time.
3. Woodsville Plantation and John and Presley Neville House, Bridgeville, Pennsylvania. The place figured prominently in the Whiskey Rebellion of 1794.
4. Oscar Getz Museum of Whiskey History, Bardstown, Kentucky.
5. West Overton Museum, Pennsylvania. Restored 19th century village.
6. Oliver Miller Homestead, S. Park, Pennsylvania. Whiskey Rebellion site.

The "Distilled Spirits Council" also lists the following operating distilleries that offer excellent tours to the public:

1. Barton Brands Distillery, Bardstown, Kentucky. Founded on this site in 1879. Has state-of-the-art Visitor Center.
2. Woodford Reserve Distillery, Versailles, Kentucky,

fully restored and designated a National Historic site.

3. Jim Beam, Clermont, Kentucky. The same family has operated the distillery for over 200 years.
4. Makers Mark, Loretto, Kentucky. Established 1805, oldest working distillery on its original site.
5. Jack Daniels. Lynchburg, TN. Oldest registered distillery in the U.S, over 140 years old.
6. George Dickel, Tullahoma, Tennessee.
7. Wild Turkey, Lawrenceville, Kentucky.
8. Buffalo Trace – Franklin County, Tennessee.

RUM

"I always keep a supply of stimulant handy in case I see a snake which I also keep handy." – W.C. Fields

In 1770, rum still ranked as the most popular distilled beverage of the period. Other fermented beverages were available, but inadequate brewing and preserving techniques yielded a product so notoriously mediocre, bitter, and flat that many people simply opted for cheap rum instead. Domestic wine was even more unpalatable, and imported wine was scarce and expensive. The only serious competition to rum was hard cider, produced domestically from the apple orchards of the northern colonies. W.J. Rorabaugh estimates that among drinking-age persons (15 years and over), the annual consumption rate in 1770 was 7.0 gallons of distilled spirits, (predominately rum), 34 gallons of hard cider, 0.2 gallons of wine, and a negligible quantity of beer. Rum and hard cider were obviously the drinks of choice.

Rum is made by fermenting and distilling the industrial waste by-product of sugar refining—molasses. The production of rum probably goes back to the 1500s. The European sugar cane plantation owners in the Caribbean encouraged the production of rum in the 1600s and 1700s. Since it was made from a waste by-product, it was very cheap. It was an unexpected windfall for the plantation owners.

The British Navy was responsible for spreading rum around the globe. Dinner on a ship in the 1600s consisted of dried peas and salt pork. Anything to help get this down was welcomed. British sailors were rationed half an imperial pint per day (10 ounces). When Admiral Sir Edward "Old Grogram" Vernon observed his deckhand's performance was dwindling, he diluted the ration with water, and divided it into two separate servings. The drink came to be known as "grog."

The name "kill-devil" was given to rum because of its

fiery taste. Almost anything and everything was added to rum to improve the flavor: cinnamon, raisins, cherries, nutmeg and nuts. American colonials were wild about a punch-like drink called "shrub," usually a barrel of orange water, raisins, honey and brandy—rum was often substituted for the brandy.

The idea of rum punch is several centuries old. The ideal recipe is a simple take on an island rhyme: "one part sour, two parts sweet, three parts strong, four parts weak." In other words, add one ounce of limejuice, two ounces of sugar cane syrup, three ounces of rum and four ounces of water. A modern version would add lots of ice and nutmeg.

In 1860, Don Facunada Bacardi in Cuba developed soft, light rum, which is popular to this day. It mixes with anything, just like vodka. Rum and coke became a major drink during WWII, even inspired a hit song by the Andrew Sisters, "Rum and Coca-Cola."

In 1770, the colonies imported four million gallons of rum and distilled another five million gallons. Of this huge amount, Americans consumed most of it themselves. Rum was also an item of trade, and Americans bartered some of it on the international market.

Rum was used in the mid 1770s in lieu of currency in what was known as the "triangle trade." Here is how it worked: Rhode Island alone had over 30 rum distilleries. A ship loaded with rum would sail for Africa where the rum would be exchanged for gold and slaves. The slaves and gold would be traded in Barbados for molasses, sugar and currency. Back in Rhode Island, the molasses would be converted to rum. The "triangle trade" ended in 1808, when the U.S. forbid the importation of slaves from Africa.

During the Revolution the British blockaded molasses and rum imports, and distillers were forced to switch from making rum to making whiskey. This resulted in a shortage of distilled spirits and the price increased significantly during the war; after the war, rum distillation resumed on a large scale. Most of these distilleries were located in seaport towns since they needed a continuing source of molasses.

In the subsequent years prior to 1800, the rum market began to slowly decline. The international market deteriorated for a variety of economic reasons, including the French and English closing their colonies to American trade. At the same time, consumption fell within the United States. Americans drank eight million gallons of rum in 1770, and by 1789, while the population had almost doubled, they drank only seven million gallons.

Erratic supplies and higher prices for rum had encouraged a shift to cider, beer and whiskey. There was also a strong feeling of nationalism sweeping the country, and imported molasses and rum were symbols of colonialism, and reminders that America was not economically self-sufficient. It was unpatriotic to depend on foreign nations or colonies for goods that could be produced here. America was searching for economic independence.

After the federal government was established in 1789, Congress imposed rum and molasses duties. In an effort to maintain the price ratio between rum and whiskey, a tax on whiskey was also established; as discussed earlier, this was very unpopular and was eventually abolished.

These higher prices hastened the decline of rum as the nation's number one distilled alcoholic drink. In 1774, prior to the Revolution, whiskey was considered a rare drink; 15 years later whiskey accounted for one-third of all distilled alcohol consumed in the United States. Rum struggled to hold on to the other two-thirds of distilled alcohol sales.

The final blow came in 1802 when Congress repealed the whiskey tax. While these government-sponsored economic measures were taking a toll on rum, particularly imported rum, cheaper whiskey was becoming better in quality, and significantly greater in availability.

In the last quarter of the 18th century, large numbers of Scotch, Irish, and Scotch Irish immigrants had landed in America. These whiskey-drinking people had been distilling grain for at least two centuries. When these people began to settle the western frontier they found conditions ideal to employ their talents: plentiful grain, pure water and an abundant supply of wood to fuel their efficient stills.

Whiskey enjoyed a meteoric rise in popularity. The per capita consumption rate of distilled spirits, aided by inexpensive, good quality and plentiful whiskey, recovered from a post war low of 5.1 gallons in 1790 to 7.2 gallons in 1800.

Rye was the first whiskey in the colonies—distilled from rye, corn and barley malt, with at least 51% of the mixture rye. Corn also made fine whiskey with about 80% of the barley malt and rye mixture being replaced by corn.

SIGNS

"When I read about the evils of drinking, I gave up reading." –
Henny Youngman

Prominent in the history of taverns in America were the early American tavern signs. Signs for taverns were used from the very beginning. The Romans and Greeks used signs depicting grapes to designate drinking establishments. Signs continued to be needed in the 17th and 18th centuries, not just as a form of advertising, but because most people could not read. In the 17th century, Louis XIV mandated that tavern keepers put up signboards throughout France.

Innkeepers were not the only ones to use signs; all trades and crafts sought signs to explain their business, and to attract customers. These signs were usually painted or carved on wood; they could be chiseled in stone, painted on tiles, modeled in clay or designed from wrought metal.

Most of these signs were pretty easily recognized: the lemon trader had a "basket of lemons," the hatter used "Hatt and Beaver," the ship's store used a "Quadrant," the chemist shop a "Mortar and Pestle."

Many of the tavern signs resulted from the familiar corruptions of generations of use; for example, "The Bag of Nails" a favorite, was originally "The Bacchanalians." The "Cat and Wheel" was the "Catherine Wheel," and still earlier, "St. Catherine's Wheel." The "Bull and Mouth" celebrates the victory of Henry VIII in "Boulogne Mouth" or "Boulogne Harbor."

Many famous English artists painted signs to make a decent living. In this country, Benjamin West painted many tavern signs in the Philadelphia vicinity. The sign he painted for the Three Crowns in Lancaster County still bears the marks of hostile bullets fired by the Continental Army at the Tory owned Inn. Several other Philadelphia taverns claimed to have signboards painted by the Peales and by Gilbert Stuart.

West also painted the sign for the Old Hat Tavern outside Philadelphia. The "Ale Bearers" sign was painted by West and pictured a man holding a glass of ale and peering through it on one side; on the other side the painting showed two porters carrying a cask.

Prior to the Revolutionary War, the British Generals Wolfe and Putnam were among the signboard favorites. During and following the War, all British symbols gave way to American eagles and heroes. Every town of any size had at least one Washington tavern, and names like "The Thistle and Crown," "Duke of Cumberland," "White Lion," "Rose & Thistle," "The King's Arms," "King's Head," "St. George and the Dragon," "Queens' Whatever" just disappeared. They were replaced with names like Franklin, Hancock, Lafayette, American Eagle and Liberty Inn. Drawings of horses, coaches, and other sporting subjects were also often used. A common tavern sign showed the American eagle holding the British lion in its claws.

In seaport towns it was common to depict a ship on the tavern sign. Every possible combination of ship and "something" was used. The "Ship and Anchor," "Ship and Bell," "Ship and Castle," "Ship and Star," "Ship and Whale," "Ship and Dock"— on and on it goes.

Many paintings of Washington appeared in his famous "Crossing the Delaware" pose. A hundred years later as the West was settled, saloons were adorned with copies of "Custer's Last Stand."

Birds, insects, and animals were frequent signboard themes. A beehive swarming with bees was popular. Often a verse appeared below the sign for those fortunate enough to be able to read.

For example:

> "Here in this hive we're all alive,
> Good liquor makes us funny.
> If you are dry, step in and try
> The flavor of our honey."

Other signboards used mugs of beer, a rider with his horse and hounds, or a coach and horses. A favorite subject for portraits, in addition to the American patriots, were Indian chiefs.

Colonial requirements usually gave the innkeeper a maximum of 30 days to put up a sign; and this was a lucrative business for artists of the time.

The signs used to identify a bar, tavern or whatever continued to change and evolve over the years. The 1800s featured names like Richardson's Canal House on the Erie Canal, The Whistle Stop on the railroad, The Hare and Hound in the country, and the names of famous people and places were used in the cities, i.e., Lincoln Tavern, Grant Bar, Custer's Place, etc.

In the first half of the 20th century things did not change very much; lots of owner's names: Harry's Bar, Joe's Tavern, Fitzgerald Snug, The Corner Bar; Cowboy Bar and Grill. Animal names were used often; Lion's Den, Bull and Bear, Brown Bear, Running Bear and Thirsty Whale, etc.

After the 1960s, bar titles changed significantly. A recent sampling turned up these off-beat creations: Psycho Suze's, Heavenly Soles, Bar Fly, The Stress Factory, Stone Pony, Hook, Line and Sinker, Urban Wildlife, Crazy Monkeys.

Irish pubs have been a fixture in this country for over 150 years. In New Jersey each year "The Irish Pubs of the Jersey Shore" sponsor an Irish Pub Tour. Now these are just some of the Irish bars in an area covering about 25 miles, and with no towns having a population over 15,000: The Dublin House, Murphy's Style Grill, Branigans, Briodys, House of Blarney, Donovan's Reef, Celtic Cottage, Gleason's, Rod's Olde Irish Tavern, Flannigan's, O'Neil's, The Claddaugh Irish Pub, Mulligan's, Kelly's, McCann's, Paddy McDonald's, Clancy's and plenty more.

48

Other names relate to the bar's location: Lobster Shanty, Crabhouse, Ocean Grill, Barnacle Bill's, Wharf Pub—all located on the water. Or in the mountains; Top of the World, Mountain View, and Hidden Valley Pub. If located at a ski resort you can count on Tips Up Lounge, The Igloo, The Lift Peak, Apres Ski, etc.

Every once in a while you will come across a new one, a really catchy creative name, even after all these years. Two women recently opened a new bar in Toronto, Canada and named it "The Cock and Tail." The décor is a cross between a bordello and a pub with red leather walls, handmade wood accents, and tiny tea lights on the tables.

HOTELS

"It is better to hide ignorance; but it is hard to do this when we relax over wine." – Heraclitus (540-480BC)

The end of the Revolution signaled another significant addition to America's drinking establishments. The first hotels appeared in the 1790s and were a large step up in both size and quality. At this time the most fashionable and comfortable taverns were located in the major cities, such as the Raleigh Tavern in Williamsburg, Virginia and the City Tavern in Philadelphia. These featured large public rooms, but sleeping quarters were small and lacked privacy. The New York City Hotel built in 1794 had 137 rooms. The bar, ballroom, public parlors, offices and library occupied the high-ceiling first and second floors.

State regulation of prices for food and drink declined gradually after the Revolution; and this enabled hotels to price the working classes out of the hotel bar. As a result, the bars in hotels became the classy places to drink; they set the standards for "proper dining." When the temperance movement took hold in the early 19th century, it was directed at saloons and taverns; hotels were excluded from criticism.

Women were welcomed at hotels while they continued to be unwelcome at taverns. Women were not always accepted at the bar in these hotels, but they did participate in celebrations and banquets at the hotel. In fact, as late as 1970, women were not welcome at the famous bar of the Biltmore Hotel in New York City. To discourage their presence whenever a woman sat down in the bar, the men began to whistle loudly until she left. Certain clubs in New York City and other cities did not permit women in the bar area until forced to admit them by legal precedents in the

1980s, i.e., the University Club of New York was the last to relent.

So, the hotel began to change things gradually. The elite tavern of the colonial period, which effectively segregated people by gender, race and class, emerged around the turn of the century as the hotel.

Boston had two very fine hotels in the early 1800s. The Lafayette Hotel was completed in 1824, just in time to do honor to the great Frenchman; later it was known as the Brigham Hotel. In 1829, The Tremont House Hotel opened in Boston and offered indoor plumbing with eight bathtubs, and eight "water closets." It also had individually locked rooms and complimentary bars of soap.

Just as today, many of the most famous bars in this country in succeeding years were located in upscale hotels.

In the late 1700s, another gathering place appeared when coffee houses began arriving on every street corner in London. The first coffee house in London opened in 1652. This coffee house trend lasted until the end of the 18th century. As with so many other customs, it did not take long for the coffee house fad to reach America.

Coffee houses in this country probably originated in Boston in 1670 when officials gave Dorothy Jones a license to sell coffee and "chuchaletto." By the beginning of the 18th century coffee houses were well established.

The Merchant's Coffee House opened at Wall and Water Streets in New York City in 1754. The London coffee house opened the same year at Front and Market streets in Philadelphia. These places became the center of trade and often served liquor, as well as coffee and tea. The Exchange Coffee House opened much later in Boston, 1808, and was seven stories high. In addition to serving hot drinks, another notable difference between coffee houses and taverns was that coffee houses were not required to provide lodging.

Now at the beginning of the 21st century, the coffee house has once again "arrived." This time it is a major force in the restaurant scene. Starbucks alone has over 2600 locations. Today's coffee houses concentrate their business on coffee flavors and do not sell alcohol.

BEGINNING OF THE 19th CENTURY

"And malt does more than Milton can do to justify God's ways to man." – A.E. Housman

The 19th century brought many changes and new ideas to the American drinking establishment. These included the expansion of the western frontier, roads and railroads, canals, the Civil War, the "Wild West," and an increasing interest in Prohibition.

In 1800, the village church and the village tavern continued to stand side by side as the two most prominent buildings in town. The great majority of men in every region were tavern goers. City men came to their neighborhood taverns daily; and in the countryside, taverns were the source of sociability for men in the dreary months of winter.

Americans continued to drink as the nation entered the 19th century, and they drank in enormous quantities. Their yearly consumption at the time of the Revolution has been estimated as the equivalent of three and one-half gallons of pure (200 proof) alcohol per person. After 1790, probably in response to anxieties generated by rapid and unsettling social change, American men began to drink even more. By 1792 licensing had been introduced and there were 2579 licensed distillers. This had risen to 14,200 distillers by 1810.

The period between 1790 and 1830 was probably the heaviest drinking time in our nation's history. There are various historical estimates of alcohol consumption based on diaries, travel reports and local histories; but a consensus would place consumption at an annual average of 5.8 gallons of absolute, pure alcohol (200 proof) for people aged 15 and over in 1790. This rose to 7.1 gallons per year in 1810, where it remained until 1830. Over half of this alcohol was in the form of distilled liquor, while the remainder was in the form of beer, wine and cider. By comparison, consumption in 1970 was 2.5 gallons of pure alcohol per person per year.

Some sources claim that consumption of distilled spirits reached a peak of 9.5 gallons per person, per year in 1830, before it began a long, continuous decline.

Since the mid 19th century, per capita consumption in the U.S. has never been much more than two gallons a year—a contrast that is even more remarkable because the proportion of the population old enough to be serious drinkers had increased significantly.

Drink was everywhere in the social world of early 19th century America. Liquor was as common as food. It was present for all occasions; weddings, birthdays, funerals, or whenever two or three neighbors gathered.

The old notion that alcohol was necessary for good health remained firmly fixed. It was common to down a glass of whiskey or other spirits before breakfast. Instead of taking coffee or tea breaks, Americans stopped every morning and afternoon at 11 o'clock ("eleveners") and 4 o'clock for drams (called draming.). A dram would equal about one and one-half ounces of whiskey—a shot. Even school children took their morning and afternoon sips of whiskey. In the evenings plenty of liquor was drunk during and after dinner to aid digestion and sleep. Before retiring one took a "strengthening" nightcap; one recipe called for "whiskey, maple syrup, nutmeg, and boiling water—the whole thing dashed with rum."

Clergymen drank between services, lawyers before going to court, judges in court, and physicians at the bedside of their patients. To do a day's work, raising a barn, or seeing a patient, without a drink was considered impossible. Drinking in taverns, although the most visible, may have accounted for no more than one-quarter of what Americans consumed.

City taverns catered to clienteles of different classes: sordid grog shops near the waterfront universally connected with brawling and prostitution; neighborhood taverns and liquor-selling groceries visited by craftsmen and clerks; well-appointed and relatively decorous places favored by substantial merchants. Taverns on busy roads often specialized in teamsters (drovers) or stagecoach passengers, while country inns took their patrons as they came.

Taverns, whether city or country, continued to be the social center of the region or neighborhood. Men came, not just to drink, but to socialize and hear the latest news. Information was available from travelers, newspapers, and a profusion of notices, advertisements and messages. These covered the walls of the taproom and included announcements of town meetings, handwritten notes offering goods for sale and warning about runaway slaves and apprentices.

Taverns accommodated women as travelers, and let out rooms for dances; but their barroom clienteles were almost exclusively male. The 18th century practice of widows often running taverns began to disappear after 1800.

Laws forbidding taverns to serve servants, apprentices, minors or slaves were on the books throughout the United States; but in most places they were not rigidly enforced. The unwritten consensus was that liquor would not be denied to those youths who did a man's work, or were accepted in the company of drinking men.

Entertainment in taverns came in a vast variety of forms, but gambling was the major feature in the early 1800s. Men played billiards, cards and rolled the dice for money. In the South, horse racing was added to the gambling menu for the upper classes. Turkey shoots and fox hunting were popular in New England and the South. The horses, riders and hounds would assemble at the tavern, and return at day's end to celebrate.

Outdoors, in addition to horse racing, the blood sports of bull baiting, and dog and cock fights were popular. In all of these events the animals fought to the death, or were severely maimed. Consequently, they were illegal everywhere and punishable by strict fines; but the laws were enforced erratically if at all. To this day, cock fights and dogfights continue to be held illegally in this country.

Public hangings often attracted large crowds and afforded taverns a large amount of business. Tavern keepers were known to hire "watchers" to keep a careful eye on the condemned prisoner in the weeks before the hanging, so that the culprit should not, by suicide, cheat them out of the day's gains. A reprieve or stay of execution might disappoint a crowd intent on witnessing the deadly drama and provoke a riot, as it did in Pembroke, New Hampshire in 1834.

American taverns were also windows on the exotic, places where traveling exhibitions, menageries and circuses stopped and put on their shows. The earliest American circus audience was not, as they became much later, gatherings of families with children in tow; rather, adult and primarily male. The shows were clearly part of a masculine world whose boundaries were defined by liquor, and the possibility of violence.

After 1800, another nuisance appeared and lasted for over 100 years as the practice of chewing tobacco became widespread. Americans took alcohol and tobacco in close association. Every tavern had its rack of pipes and floor liberally stained with tobacco juice. Spittoons were provided in the more meticulous establishments; but spitting and tobacco juice were everywhere.

Some of the most profound changes in the history of our country took place between 1790 and 1830. Almost every aspect of American life underwent change, much of it major change. It is no coincidence that this same period represents the time of the heaviest alcohol consumption in our history. Change leads to anxiety, and anxiety leads to drinking.

The single most important change, with the most far-reaching consequences, was the rapid growth in population. During the period 1790-1810, the population grew from four million to over seven million.

All of these people had to find land to live on, since the U.S. was still an agrarian society. This led to pioneers heading for the West, over the Appalachian Mountains. In 1790, only

100,000 of the 4 million Americans lived in the West. By 1810, 1 million of the 7 million Americans lived there.

At the same time the urban areas of the country grew at a rapid rate. In 1790, there were only eight cities with populations over 5,000; by 1830, there were forty-five cities with over 5,000 people. And these cities were not all clustered along the seacoast as in 1790; they had spread west as far as Cincinnati. In addition, of course, the large cities grew much larger. Between 1790 and 1830, Philadelphia grew from 40,000 to 160,000 and New York City from 30,000 to 200,000.

All this growth over such a short period of time just overwhelmed public services such as sanitation, law and order, and community improvements.

Another historic change occurring during this 40-year period involved improvements in transportation. Steamboats appeared, canals were built——notably the Erie Canal finished in 1825—and by 1840 the railroad began to take control of transportation. This changed the US economy from a regional base to a national market. The result of being able to ship goods economically caused a surge in manufacturing.

The country began to shift from being a farm-based one to being a manufacturing- or factory-based one. Large-scale factories were producing textiles, paper, glass, pottery, sugar, dyes, etc. This caused a change in the life style of the average family. In place of the relatively slow, secure and quiet pace of an agricultural job; the worker was now engaged in tasks that were dull, repetitious, with more time spent away from home.

There is no doubt the number of taverns grew tremendously. A few examples demonstrate the point. In fast-growing Rochester, New York, a result of the Erie Canal, in 1827 there were 100 establishments licensed to sell liquor in a town with a population of 8,000. This is one tavern for every 80 inhabitants regardless of age. Street directories for typical church-going New England towns list far more licensed drinking establishments than meetinghouses.

Records for my hometown of Olean, New York, in 1877,

show that every store on the north side of the main street was, with the exception of one, a saloon. The one exception was a grocery store. This has changed, but not completely. On a recent cruise up and down the two main intersecting streets, Union and State streets, my wife and I counted a total of 36 establishments that obviously served alcoholic beverages.

THE STAGECOACH TAVERN

"When you have lost your inns, you may drown your empty selves, for you will have lost the heart of England." Poet Hilaire Belloc

By 1800, America had progressed from pack trails to wagon roads, to turnpikes or pikes, post roads and toll roads. The stagecoach routes between cities brought a need for taverns to furnish food and lodging for travelers and their horses.

For example, on the road from Albany to Schenectady to Utica, New York a tavern was located every mile—and it was not enough. There were fifty taverns within 50 miles. A tavern might have as many as 100 horse stables. In 1805, Haverhill, New Hampshire became a "staging center." This transformed a sleepy farm village into a town with many taverns. Over 150 passengers could be lodged overnight. Bliss's Tavern was one of the first in Haverhill and the rooms and food were cheap, the money was made on the liquor.

The stagecoach inn remained popular until 1850, when the arrival of the train ended its role in American travel. Stage lines are said to have been running in 1733 between New York and Philadelphia, by way of Perth Amboy and Burlington, New Jersey. There is an authentic record that in November 1756, "a new stage left John Butler's 'Sign of the Death of the Fox' in Philadelphia for New York City." After 1785, stage lines connected New York with Albany, Boston, and Philadelphia. Stages left both ends of the route twice a week. The trip between New York and Albany took three days in summer, and four days in winter; a day's journey lasted from five o'clock in the morning until ten o'clock at night.

The stages on all routes were drawn by four horses, and could accommodate up to 12 passengers. The fare was four pence per mile, and 14 pounds of luggage was carried free.

These early stagecoaches were primitive. An early traveler between Philadelphia and Washington in 1795 described the vehicle as follows:

"The vehicle was a long car with four benches, three of these in the interior held nine passengers; a tenth passenger was seated by the side of the driver on the front bench. Three large leather curtains suspended to the roof; one on each side, and a third behind; were rolled up or lowered at the pleasure of the passengers. There was no space for luggage, each person being expected to stow his things as he could under his seat or legs. There were no backs to support or relieve us during a long and fatiguing journey over a newly and ill-made road."

It was no wonder these people were glad to stop at a stagecoach inn at the end of the day. The stagecoach driver's life was a miserable one; he accommodated to the lonely life away from home by drinking pretty much all day long. He would have a drink in the A.M. just to help face the day ahead. Whenever he stopped to water the horses was another occasion to have a drink. Most drivers kept a bottle on the seat beside them. The driver could not leave his team unattended while it was attached to the coach. To ride the stage coach passengers were required to board early in the day, usually 5 A.M., but sometimes as early as 3 A.M. A trip from Olean, New York to Buffalo in 1840, a distance of 70 miles, took two and a half days.

Road conditions were terrible. The usual width of the road was eight feet, hemmed in on both sides by great forests; roads were a continuous mud hole in the spring and dusty ruts in the summer. Streams were not bridged, swamps were everywhere, and sparse settlement made travel lonely and perilous. Delays were frequent, resulting from equipment breakdowns, impassable road conditions, inclement weather, and even because of droves of cattle, pigs, etc. being driven to market.

Over the next three decades, the "stage wagons" became much more comfortable. It was not until 1827 that the first Concord Stage was made. The stage was suspended from the frame by strong leather straps, which gave riders some protection from the jolting of the roads. Passengers entered through a door on the side. Nine passengers rode inside the coach on three rows of seats. A tenth passenger rode outside next to the driver. These new stages soon became popular all over the country.

In Farmington, Connecticut stands what is probably the oldest stagecoach inn open continuously as such in the United States, the Elm Tree Inn, a tavern since 1660 or at the latest, 1670.

There were two types of taverns serving travelers at the beginning of the 19th century in America. A stagecoach tavern was considered upscale from a drover's or wagoner's inn. In fact, if a stagecoach inn catered to drovers it would soon lose its reputation and the stages would no longer stop there. It is said that when one inn was practically forced one night to shelter a drover, he was accepted only on condition that he leave early the next morning before the coach guests should see him. Inns were class oriented, and drovers were at the bottom of the list.

A drover, or teamster, or wagoner, brought goods from the countryside to the market and there were long lines of drover's pungs coming toward a tavern on winter nights; and in summer, the progress of herds going toward Boston might be followed by clouds of dust they stirred up.

One hundred horses could be stabled in the barns; and 2-300 cattle could graze around the tavern. There were pens for sheep; and turkeys, driven in flocks through the roads to Boston markets just before Thanksgiving, would roost in the trees, and on the tavern and its out buildings.

Drovers used herding dogs and 13 miles was a day's journey for a pig drover. Taverns rented enclosed pastures for the animals and the drovers slept on the floor of the tavern or three to a bed. It might be 100 miles from the farm to the market. These sleeping accommodations in taverns were often dirty and insect ridden. Feather beds and straw ticks readily accommodated bed bugs, fleas, etc.

The Munroe Tavern built in 1695 is now a museum in

Lexington, Massachusetts. Large rows of beds used to be set up in the dance hall, for this was a drover's tavern.

In 1772, when stages began running between New York City and Boston (the second stage line in America), the Williams Tavern was one of three stage stops between Boston and Worcester, Massachusetts. The tavern on this site was constructed in 1662. The original structure was destroyed by fire during an Indian raid; but was quickly rebuilt and the building with many modifications, still stands.

Throughout the U.S. there are many fine examples of stagecoach inns still in use today. The excellent book "Early American Inns and Taverns," by Elise Lathrop, published in 1926, provides historical information and photographs of a large collection of taverns on a state by state basis.

Usually these inns were two stories high with an attic and windows in the gable-ends. The building would be square with a long porch across the front from which two doors opened. Two doors were typical of most inns in early America, and this remained fairly standard into the 1960s. One door always led into the taproom or barroom, the other led into a hall which opened to the inn, parlor, or in some cases the family living quarters.

Well into the 20th century, neighborhood bars had two entrances. Again, one always opened into the barroom, the other into an area furnished with tables and chairs, or booths. In this area customers could bring their dates or families, order food and drinks, and listen to music or enjoy a conversation.

In Olean, New York, in the 1950s, on cold winter evenings we teenagers often spent hours in various bars drinking beer and playing shuffleboard. Since the drinking age at the time was 18, and we were 16 and 17, we were never allowed to venture into the barroom side of the establishment.

Inns in New England were almost always constructed of wood, while in Pennsylvania stone was the primary construction material for inns and taverns.

Wooden construction consisted of planks up to two feet

wide, enormous beams, narrow steep stairs with low ceilings. Cellars often had cobblestone floors; and the kitchens were whitewashed (a mixture of lime or chalk with water). And, of course, fireplaces were large and numerous. All inns had to have stables for horses both the stagecoach horses, and the horses of the overnight guests.

The stone taverns in Pennsylvania had walls two feet thick. The Sun Inn, with its stone walls, was constructed in 1757-1760 near Bethlehem, Pennsylvania. It was two stories high, with a mansard roof, a reception room 24 x 16 feet, offices and kitchen on the lower floor; a dining room 37 x 18 feet, and three suites, each consisting of a sitting-room and two bed chambers on the second floor. This inn was quite elegant for its day and was built by the Moravians, a religious sect from Eastern Europe.

Oziel Smith opened The Eagle House Tavern on Main Street in Williamsville, New York in 1827 with the slogan "Bird, Beef and Bottle, with a bed for the weary traveler." A hot meal cost 25 cents and a bed for the night was10 cents. The Conestoga Wagon Line, along with two passenger stagecoach lines stopped here once a day on their way to the newly prospering city of Buffalo. The inn was a nightly stopover between Buffalo and Batavia.

Oziel Smith was an experienced builder who used his nearby quarry to provide the two-foot thick limestone foundation that The Eagle House continues to sit on today. The lumber came from his wooded property, and the saw mill was located steps away near a waterfall on Ellicott Creek.

Close examination of this inn that continues to operate every day of the year, reveals the original workmanship including the carved ceiling as well as a ballroom with a "spring floor' on the second story. The first floor has the typical barroom on one side; and the dining area in the next room. The Eagle House boasts of having the longest continuously held liquor license in New York State.

An old almanac cited 21 inns in the 60 miles between

Lancaster, Pennsylvania and Philadelphia, but a later authority gives the number as 66. Some of the names for these inns are memorable: The Rising Sun in Schuylkill; The White Lamb at Wynnefield; Sorrel Horse in Radnor; The Plough in Geiger's Mills; The Blue Ball in Daylesford; Steamboat in Chester; Barley Sheaf in Jenkintown; States Arms in Sudsbury; General Wayne in Collegeville.

The early taverns in the frontier states of Ohio, Kentucky and Tennessee usually began as log cabins chinked with mortar. They would have two large rooms on the ground floor with a half-story above. This served as both the proprietor's dwelling and a tavern for overnight guests.

As late as 1840-1850, these taverns had no bathing facilities. Unheated sleeping rooms had small windows, corded beds; and for mattresses, sacks filled with straw. In very cold weather warming pans might be used; sheets and pillowcases were provided but these were not always clean. Often these taverns were so crowded that the guests drew lots to see who slept on the kitchen floor. Tallow candles furnished the lighting until replaced by kerosene lamps.

In addition to all the normal functions performed by a typical bar in the 1800s, the following story must be added as a historical landmark.

Work on the Erie Canal in New York State commenced in 1817. Progress in clearing the land and digging the ditch was satisfactory; but the engineers had not found a way to seal the spaces between the neatly arranged stones lining the sides of the excavation, the locks, culverts and aqueducts. The available common quicklime in use at the time was unstable, breaking down under any sustained pressure. This required constant relining of the surfaces.

A young engineer working on the project, Canvass White, heard about some contractors working on the canal near Syracuse that had come upon a limestone that did not disintegrate when it became wet.

All the important people responsible for constructing the

canal set up a meeting at Elisha Carey's barroom in the Village of Chittenango, 20 miles east of Syracuse, New York. An experiment was set up in the middle of the bar. A handful of moist mortar made from the local limestone was mixed with sand, rolled into a ball, and placed in a bucket of water overnight. When the group met at the bar the next morning the ball was as hard as a rock. The mortar problem had been solved at Elisha Carey's bar, and after considerable celebration, the canal construction continued. The Erie Canal, a tremendous engineering feat at the time, was completed in October 1825. This 365-mile canal between Albany and Buffalo, New York wedded Lake Erie and the Hudson River, opening transportation from the Great Lakes to the Atlantic Ocean.

Of course, the Erie Canal and many others built at the time required the construction of another type of tavern – the "canal house." These places sprung up in every village along the canal route; especially near canal locks. Towns like Brookport, Lockport, Spencerport and Fairport along the Erie Canal have fine examples of "canal houses" that continue to operate today.

In the 10 years after 1830, Americans saw the "Railway" as the most striking sign of change in a time filled with changes. There were just 700 miles of track in 1835 and only 3,000 miles in 1840 and 9,000 miles by 1850. By 1900 there were over 193,000 miles of track crisscrossing the United States.

The first steam passenger railroad in this country, the New Castle and Frenchtown Rail Road, in 1832, replaced the stagecoaches in Pennsylvania.

A stagecoach under ideal conditions might average eight or nine miles per hour. The railroad was twice as fast, and could keep going over long distances. Disadvantages included noise and dirt, ash, and cinders. Passengers disembarked dirty and half-deaf from the noise of the wheels on the rails and the engine which pulled several cars.

The stagecoach was doomed and disappeared within 20 years; the stagecoach tavern began to disappear along with it. The various inns and taverns associated with the canal system suffered a similar fate.

Eventually almost every town, regardless of size, had a tavern or hotel located close to the railroad station. These were needed to accommodate travelers waiting for connecting trains, business people staying the night, or just guests visiting the town. Once again the tavern had to change and move to accommodate new modes of travel; but its basic characteristics remained the same. As the Irish say, "Ah, it's the same, but different."

FOOD

"Reminds me of my safari in Africa. Somebody forgot the corkscrew and we lived for days with nothing but food and water."—W.C. Fields

The food served in taverns and inns varied enormously and was dependent, not only on the quality of the establishment and the geographical location, but also upon the time of year. Summer afforded the opportunity to offer fresh fruits and vegetables. These included wild strawberries, melons, asparagus, beans, potatoes, corn, etc. Poultry and eggs were served along with beef and fish and were accompanied by coffee, tea, wine, and brandy. Desserts consisted of pastries and puddings and included apple and mince pies.

As you traveled farther west to the frontier states of Indiana, Wisconsin, Kentucky and the Midwest, the food became plainer. Food was abundant, but vegetables were absent. There were parried chickens, quail, pigeons and pies for dinner. The pies were often made of green tomatoes, or dried pumpkin or apples. Buckwheat cakes with maple syrup or sorghum were served for breakfast. One large "salt-cellar" placed in the middle of the long table served everyone.

Black and red currants, high bush cranberries, plums, crabapples, grapes, strawberries, and raspberries, all grew wild. Venison was also frequently offered, and was obtained by trading with the Indians. Winter, of course, changed the menu, and it became a monotonous serving of meat for all three meals each day.

A busy tavern might serve up to 200 meals in a single day. A menu from an inn in Kentucky sounds quite good for the early 1800s: "venison steak, bass fried in corn meal, moist-fattened bacon, cured with a hickory wood fire, snap beans cooked with green corn, pone bread from the skillet on the hearth, and cider, rum, French brandy and home-made wines."

1830

"A woman drove me to drinking and I never had the courtesy to thank her." —W.C. Fields

As the 19ᵗʰ century progressed into the '30s and '40s, several major drinking changes were taking place. First was a significant effort at temperance; second was the immigration from Europe—bringing with it changing drinking tastes; third was the settlement of the West.

First, look at the temperance movement.

As discussed earlier, the beginning years of the new American republic were marked by the prodigious consumption of alcoholic beverages. Being drunk was seen in early American society as a sign of privilege. To have the time and resources to be "drunk as a Lord" carried a message about one's social standing. Public displays of drunkenness were, however, rare, largely due to the habit of taking one's drink little by little – a certain tolerance was developed.

Starting first thing in the morning with a whiskey or bitter rum, stopping at the tavern for a "nip" on the way to work, a mid-morning break, more drinks in mid-afternoon and at the early evening supper. Then of course, the remainder of the evening was spent either at home or in the tavern discussing the day's events around the fireside, while drinking copious amounts of cider, whiskey, rum or gin.

In addition to alcohol being a regular part of the normal day, it played an important role in every major occasion; dances, county fairs, christenings, race meetings and weddings. It was dispensed by politicians to those they hoped would vote for them; it was even given to juries by defendants in court hearings.

Children were given alcohol, and boys in adolescence imitated their fathers by drinking in taverns as soon as they felt they could get away with it. A boy of 12 might wander into a bar at 11:00 A.M. and be served a bittered brandy without anyone blinking an eye. Women's drinking was less visible in the taverns, but not so at social gatherings and in the home. To refuse a drink was to offend the hand of hospitality and insult the host or hostess.

At this time, Americans consumed more than five gallons of liquor per capita, the highest level in the history of this country. In 1810 Louisville, Kentucky shipped 250,000 gallons of whiskey up the Ohio River; by 1822 the volume swelled to 2,250,000 gallons.

Excess was the mother of Prohibition, as it has been ever since. Although drinking remained a powerful force in many parts of the United States, the American way of drunkenness began to lose ground as early as the mid-1820s.

As described earlier, Dr. Benjamin Rush had begun to comment on the effects of alcohol on health as early as 1784.

All this alcohol consumption eventually provoked a potent reaction. It first gathered momentum in the Northeast, and some New England clergymen had campaigned in their own communities as early as 1810; but their concerns took an organized impetus with the founding of the American Temperance Society in 1826.

Energized in the past by a concern for social order, in part by evangelical piety, temperance reformers popularized a radically new way of looking at alcohol. The "good creature" became "demon rum." National and state societies generated an enormous output of anti-liquor tracts, and hundreds of local temperance societies were founded to press the cause, first, of moderation in drink, but increasingly of total abstinence from liquor. It is important to note that one thing the temperance movement was never about was temperance. From its inception it was a call for unequivocal abstinence because it believed there is no such thing as moderation or restraint in the use of intoxicants.

The temperance movement provided two interesting concepts. First, it provided the Christian Churches a method to prohibit alcohol in the name of God; and secondly, it managed to shift the moral emphasis away from the individual's culpability for his own actions while under the influence, and onto the substance itself. A drunken laborer who frittered away the family's income on boozing was a wayward soul in need of guidance.

By 1829, there were over 1,000 temperance societies in America. In the 1830s in pulpits, pamphlets, and medical journals, total prohibition was being openly advocated.

The Washington Society founded in 1840, and whose members were all reformed drunks, contributed significantly to the temperance crusade, along with the Methodist Church.

Religious fervor took over and equated drunkenness with damnation, and temperance with salvation. With God enlisted to the colors, the movement descended on village and town, waving placards outside saloons, singing soul-saving hymns, and urging all to sign "the Pledge."

The "Cold Water Pledge" was absolute, banning not only ardent spirits, but also malt liquors, wine and cider. Children were organized into "Cold Water Armies" to carry banners in parades.

In addition to its core concern for the health and welfare of working families, the temperance movement leadership had a motive for making working-class families more willing to participate in the capitalistic economy by encouraging them to manage their time more effectively, at considerable cost to their established patterns of sociability.

Organized temperance reform was sharply limited along geographical lines. Temperance societies were enormously powerful in New England, New York, New Jersey and Pennsylvania. More than three-quarters of all recorded "pledges" came from these states. In the south and west, and in the working-class neighborhoods of the larger cities, the temperance campaign rarely reshaped community life. In these places the temperance folks, or "dries" as they were known, were regarded as "a bunch of ugly women, henpecked husbands, and three-dollar preachers."

Americans responded to this barrage of persuasion by

drastically decreasing their consumption of alcohol. By 1840 it had declined by more than two-thirds to less than one and one-half gallons per capita. Country storekeepers gave up the sale of spirits, local authorities cut down the number of licenses, and farmers even abandoned hard cider and cut down their orchards.

By 1855, over one million people had signed the "pledge of abstinence." Temperance agitation on the legal front reached its peak in the 1850s, and began in Maine with statewide prohibition of public drunkenness, not private drinking. By 1855, 13 states had adopted, so called "Maine Laws."

All this effort to abolish alcohol had a profound effect on the village tavern. Without moving physically, the taverns lost their place at the center of community life. A few taverns became citadels of a newly defined respectability. They gave up their rum and whiskey selling to be transformed into "Temperance Hotels" where water, coffee, and tea were the only beverages available. Many taverns in the Northeast simply disappeared.

The campaigns of the teetotalers may not have been decisive in converting the greater part of the working class to abstinence; but they succeeded, perhaps forever, to wrest from the pub the status inscribed in its original name; the "public house." Pubs and taverns were an adjunct of the home, in which working people mingled with their neighbors and colleagues more freely than any other form of socialization allowed. By condemning the taverns as sinks of selfish excess, the temperance advocates destroyed the edifice of working-class sociality. The movement succeeded in placing the pubs beyond the pale of respectable social life.

When the prohibition movement receded and the tavern returned to favor, the practice of public drinking had changed. The tavern stopped being a seamless part of everyday behavior, and became just one of the leisure activities to which, implicitly, there were always more wholesome alternatives.

Some people tended to go to the tavern as an act of defiance, and intentionally drank to get drunk. More than ever, the drinking establishments became totally male.

Horace Greely wrote: "Our consumers of strong drink had diminished to a class of Americans, where previously they were the whole people," as the temperance movement pecked away at the moral status of communal drinking.

By the end of the 19th century, the wholesome tavern of the turn of the century had turned into a saloon full of prostitution, "crimping" (the practice of drugging customers so they could be robbed and dumped into the street), illegal gambling, and political graft. The very names of Bowery Saloons in New York City shouted their defiance in the face of cultured Manhattan society: The Flea Bag, The Hell Hole, The Dump, The Morgue, The Inferno, The Slide (probably New York's first gay bar.)

Against the assault on the American tavern, and drinking in general, arrived a counter-balancing event—European immigration.

By the mid 1850s, it looked like the temperance movement had won the battle, and the country was definitely going dry. Then, dramatically the first great temperance movement in this country lost momentum, and one by one the states, except Maine, repealed their Prohibition Laws. The reason was more pressing issues had arisen, slavery and ultimately the Civil War; war once again became a time of excessive drinking. Also, a number of European studies had shown that alcohol, while dangerous in excess, was not harmful in moderation. By the time the Civil War began in 1861, Prohibition had collapsed as a major public issue.

The Civil War period allowed taverns to operate with few constraints and many were unlicensed establishments of dubious reputation. The Temperance movement would return to America again in the 1870s. The Women's Christian Temperance Union (WCTU) was founded in Cleveland, Ohio in December 1874.

IMMIGRATION 1840-1900

"Water taken in moderation cannot hurt anyone." – Mark Twain

In the first half of the 19th century, the U.S. witnessed a wave of mass migrations from Europe. The impact on drinking patterns, customs and attitudes of this floodtide of immigrants was significant.

The Irish were the largest single group of pre-Civil War immigrants. Almost two million Irish landed here between 1830 and 1860. They were fleeing poverty, British oppression, and, during the 1840s, the Great Famine. These people were poor, uneducated and unskilled. A few moved inland and south; but most stayed on the East Coast in the port cities of Boston, New York, and Philadelphia. These people were impoverished, broken and bewildered. They were offered the menial jobs of digging canals and building railroads—they provided a cheap and plentiful labor supply for the industrializing Northern economy. Crowded into squalid tenements, it was a hard life; and it was made more difficult by social discrimination. The Irish were happy to get three meals a day and some sort of shelter.

In addition to being poor and unskilled, the Irish were Roman Catholic. Most of them clung to a personal value system rooted in deference to the Church. The United States was largely a Protestant nation, and had always mistrusted anything connected to the Roman Catholic Church. The result was widespread and large-scale discrimination. Some of the larger cities had anti-Catholic rioting prior to the Civil War. Serious efforts were made to exclude the Irish from the mainstream politics, society and economy of the day. The infamous "No Irish Need Apply" signs were commonplace.

Responding to this hostility, the Irish began to resist Americanization. They "circled the wagons" and looked to themselves for support and protection. The result was their own parochial grade schools, high schools and colleges. This was expanded to include hospitals, social clubs and militia regiments. And when they entered the political arena, it was in large, solid voting blocs controlled by the Irish ward politicians.

One of the customs that came under special scrutiny from the American born, largely Protestant, middle and upper classes was the Irish reputation for heavy drinking. In Ireland, heavy drinking had been an integral part of life rooted in the social structure known as the "bachelor group." The practice of sub-dividing land equally among sons had reached a point that parcels were too small to support families. Their solution, particularly during the Great Famine, was to delay marriage and immigrate to America. As a result, the overwhelming majority of Irish immigrants were individuals without intact families. The bachelor drinking group became their primary social unit. Hard drinking with the boys not only became a way of demonstrating one's Irishness, but also provided a sense of ethnic identification. They drank hard to assert their Irishness.

Popular opinion held that the Irish and liquor were virtually synonymous. They fit the image well from Irish saloonkeepers, to politicians, and to the all-too-often Irish drunk.

Another large group of immigrants arrived from Germany during the period 1830-1860. Almost 900,000 arrived, followed by another three million before the end of the century. The Germans were spared much of the prejudice directed at the Irish. Many Germans were skilled workers who took the better jobs denied the Irish. Others had the financial means to acquire farms or open their own businesses; in addition, fewer of the Germans were Catholic.

However, the Germans, like the Irish, brought their own traditional drinking habits with them. They drank beer; but not the warm heavy brew, mostly ale, of the colonial period. Germans drank "lager beer" made from water, hops and malt. The term "lager" means "to lay away"; their lager beer was allowed to age to a mellower flavor than American beers – "to ripen" as the Germans would say.

Johann Wagner, from Bavaria, introduced lager beer in this country. This eventually led to Pilsner beer, a cleaner and lighter lager. Alcohol content in these beers ran between 3.5 and 8.25%. German brewers began arriving in the U.S. in the 1840s. Since distribution costs were high, local, family-oriented breweries dotted the landscape. Cities with large German populations, such as St. Louis, Cincinnati and Milwaukee experienced a boom in brewery construction. By 1840, there were over 140 breweries in the U.S. The Yuengling Brewery in Pottsville, Pennsylvania was founded in 1829. It is still in operation, 177 years later, and is run by the fifth generation of the same family.

Beer has been synonymous with Milwaukee since 1844 when Jacob Best emigrated from Germany, and opened the Empire Brewery. Capt. Frederick Pabst married Best's granddaughter, and eventually took over the brewery—resulting in Pabst Blue Ribbon beer, a major brand for 75 years. Milwaukee, with its proximity to cheap water and abundant grain, coupled with a large German population, became the beer capital of the U.S.

Other German immigrants followed Jacob Best— Frederick Miller, Joseph Schlitz, and Valentine Blatz started their own breweries. By the late 1800s there were over 80 breweries in Milwaukee. This abundance of beer and beer drinkers led to the establishment of some wonderful bars and restaurants. Some continue to this day, for example the century-old Karl Maders which serves sauerkraut, wiener schnitzel and link sausage from Usinger's sausage factory located across the street. Karl Raatches is another long time favorite for German food and beer in Milwaukee. And, of course, one of the major brands, Miller beer, is still headquartered in Milwaukee.

Italians formed another significant group of immigrants in the 1800s, but intoxication was not a problem. Some feel this was a result of the Italian custom of drinking wine and treating it as food. Every meal back in Italy had to have wine; but wine was only drunk at meals. Italians drank very little hard liquor since it was not recognized as food.

The French, on the other hand, did not consider wine as food. Wine and other alcoholic drinks, i.e., brandy, were drunk at mid-day breaks, or in the late evening, not just at meals. As a result, the French were frequently more intoxicated than some other ethnic groups.

Jewish people formed another large segment of the U.S. immigrant population. Jewish-Americans were rarely inebriated. It was the custom of Jewish immigrants to treat alcohol as an ingredient of religious ceremonies. In addition, Jews were partially insulated from the anxieties of their minority status through the creation and maintenance of various Jewish institutions.

These immigrant groups played a major role as the bar scene changed in the second half of the 19th century. Despite the progressive increase in per capita beer consumption during the latter part of the 19th century, drinking in America had become as erratic as its restless and heterogeneous population. Both drinking and abstinence became closely identified with a specific social class, religion, and ethnic group. For example, middle- and upper class Protestants generally saw total abstinence as a symbol of respectability; and as a means to achieve health, success, and happiness. Books on popular manners and advice consistently associated temperance with such virtues as industry and thrift.

Saloons appeared in the growing urban centers, especially in the slum areas where opposition to Prohibition legislation among expanding ethnic populations was especially strong. In addition to serving alcohol, once again the saloon provided a convenient meeting place for groups of working men. The backrooms and halls were frequently used by social clubs, labor unions, fraternal lodges, and other organizations. Saloon halls also hosted dances and weddings and christening receptions, especially for immigrant groups. Other attractions included the notorious "free lunch," which was provided only because the law required that food be served in drinking establishments.

It wasn't long before the local tavern took on a flavor based on race, religion or country of origin. Gone was the tavern of colonial days frequented by everyone in town on an equal basis.

Now the abstinence group looked down upon the tavern while the drinking group looked back in defiance. The tavern became the "saloon," not always a respectable place, and not always frequented by respectable people.

By 1860, consumption of hard liquor in the U.S. had stabilized at a level of about two gallons of pure alcohol per capita (for every man, woman and child in the country). This was not considered heavy consumption. The German drinking rate was twice that of the U.S. and the French drank four times as much as the U.S. population.

The saloon once again became the place to socialize. Beer drinking was associated with being German, whiskey with being Irish, and wine with being Italian. These associations were used as a basis of race, class, and religious discrimination; which separated the "unwashed" immigrants from the "native" Americans. Native in this case does not mean the native Indians, but the early English immigrants whose descendants considered themselves natives.

The word saloon replaced the terms "alehouse," "tavern," "public house," "pub," "tap-room," etc., around the 1840s, and came into wide use in 1850s with the spread of the western saloons. The word "saloon" comes from the French word "salon" meaning large room or hall used for public meetings or entertainment. The idea was to bestow a bit of respectability on the drinking establishments at a time when it was once again coming under heavy criticism.

By the end of the 19th century just about every bar from coast to coast was called a saloon. Unfortunately, the word had come to conjure up visions of filth, crime, vice and drunkenness.

CIVIL WAR YEARS

"Find out what brand of whiskey he drinks so I can send some to my other generals." — *Abraham Lincoln's response to a delegation of Congressmen condemning General Ulysses S. Grant as a failure and a drunkard.*

Whiskey was scarce and valuable during the Civil War. In addition to helping men face the awfulness of the battlefield and its aftermath, whiskey often served as the only anesthetic available. Although quinine and laudanum were used, few other medicines were available in the mid-1800s.

The Confederate troops were worse off than the Union soldiers because the South declared prohibition on a state-by-state basis, claiming all the grain was needed for food. The black market price for whiskey went from 25 cents per gallon to $35 per gallon.

The term "bootlegger," so widely used during the 1920s, probably dates to the Civil War when peddlers who sold illicit booze to soldiers hid the bottles in the tops of their boots.

Following the Civil War, General Grant served two terms as President, both marred by corruption involving taxes on whiskey. Close friends of Grant in the government were accused of accepting cash from distillers, and allowing the distillers to avoid paying the whiskey tax. Grant was not a big fan of the White House, and he would go to the lobby of the Willard Hotel almost every night for a drink and a cigar. People would wait in the lobby and then talk to him about what they needed. They became known as "lobbyists."

Many regiments in the Union Army were composed exclusively of members from Irish or German backgrounds. The German regiments were frequently accompanied by their own beer wagon.

Taverns, of course, once again played a major role in the Civil War. They served as headquarters, hospitals, and hiding places. Some were used as stations on the Underground Railroad transporting Southern slaves to freedom in the North.

The Fairfield Inn in Fairfield, Pennsylvania dating from 1757 offers a self-guided tour of the property. Visitors can view the room where fugitive slaves first stopped on their quest for freedom. You can relax over a drink and dinner in this cozy tavern near a portrait of Thaddeus Stevens, the abolitionist attorney, who frequented the Inn.

In Mount Joy, Pennsylvania the catacombs below Bube's Brewery were used not only to age beer, but to hide escaped slaves. The brewery was built in the mid 1800s by Alois Bube, a German immigrant, and operated until Prohibition. The brewery is 40 feet below street level, beneath a Victorian Hotel that also houses three restaurants.

The Weatherfield Tavern in Weatherfield, Vermont was an Underground Railway Station throughout the War, helping slaves escape to Canada.

Gettysburg, Pennsylvania, scene of the most famous battle of the Civil War, has many taverns operating today that served in various roles during the battle. The historic Farmworth House Inn on Baltimore Street dates from 1810, and the walls have over 100 bullet holes from the three-day siege in 1863. The menu recreates the dining experience one would have enjoyed in the Civil War area. Balderry Inn, circa 1812, was used as a hospital during the battle, July 3, 4, 5, 1863.

The Battlefield Bed and Breakfast was occupied by Union artillery and cavalry units. The James Gettys Hotel, built in 1803, served as both a tavern and a hospital while the battle raged. The Herr Tavern and Publick House, 1816, has four dining rooms decorated with antiques and lanterns. The inn served as the first Confederate hospital during the battle.

The Springhouse Tavern at the Dobbin House is the oldest building in Gettysburg, circa 1776. In the cellar of a barn, this former slave hideout and Civil War hospital takes diners to another era. The hideout for the escaping slaves features an ingenious space created between floors. Try the Philadelphia

Fire House Punch, said to be the favorite cocktail of our founding fathers.

The Inn at Narrow Passage, Woodstock, Virginia, circa 1740, was Confederate general Stonewall Jackson's headquarters in 1862.

SETTLING THE WEST – FRONTIER SALOONS

"The problem with some people is that when they're not drunk, they're sober." – *William Butler Yeats*

Of all the bars in the history of the United States, from colonial taverns to topless dives, thanks to the American movie and television industry, the western saloon is undoubtedly the most famous.

Similar to colonial days, the saloon was often the first public building in town and the town's only club—a refuge from frontier hardship that served almost every human need. The saloon was all things to all men. It was an eatery, bath and comfort station (the only bath in town), hotel, stable, gambling den, barbershop, courtroom, church, political center, post office, sports arena, funeral parlor, library, news exchange, theatre, city hall, employment agency, museum, trading post, grocery and ice cream parlor.

The first western saloon, truly deserving the name, flourished in the Rocky Mountains a generation before the existence of roads and the coming of the Conestoga wagon. It was set up in 1822 in a place called Brown's Hole—in a spot where Wyoming, Colorado, and Utah meet. Brown's Hole flourished for 18 years catering to trappers, etc. Then the beaver disappeared along with the popular beaver hats—and Brown's Hole disappeared.

The first saloons were typically rudimentary buildings; some were just "dugouts" in the side of a hill. Others consisted of little more than a shack with a row of barrels for a bar. Many of the very early western saloons were located in tents, usually a Civil War tent. There were also whiskey peddlers who operated out of a wagon or a crude tent; these were often called "road ranches." The usual progression was settler's log cabins, "road ranches," and then the saloon, followed by the fancy hotel barrooms when the railroad arrived.

The first public building in the town was usually the

saloon—churches came later, often much later; so, the saloon often doubled as the church. Funerals and wakes were held in the saloon—the undertaker had his shop in a corner of the room.

The western saloon was initially modeled after New England inns and taverns; but quickly adapted to the social needs and drinking styles of the frontier. Adorned by paintings of naked women, or Custer's last stand, the saloon's décor mirrored the unrefined and aggressive characteristics of its patrons.

Western saloons were pretty much "men only," except for the "nymphs of the prairie," and the "waiter girls," who in a way enhanced the maleness of the place.

On the mining frontier, Leadville, Colorado, high in the Rocky Mountains, west of Denver, became by far the largest and wealthiest urban center. Large deposits of both gold and silver attracted thousands of people; and by 1882 it was the largest town in Colorado. It was reported that at the end of 1880, the $4 million in trade done annually by the city's 249 saloons exceeded that of any other business except banking and mining.

Here's a description of Leadville's "Board of Trade Saloon" outlined in Chapter 2 of Elliot West's book "The Saloon on the Rocky Mountain Mining Frontier."

"Just inside the door was a counter displaying cigars for sale. To the right was a long bar with a large diamond-dust mirror on the back wall. At tables opposite the bar, men drank and played cards. In the back, a band played and men risked their hard-earned wages in games of faro and keno. Kerosene lamps provided the lighting, and the decorations ranged from stuffed deer heads to paintings of muscular boxers and nude women." This was a typical saloon of the late 1880s.

The saloons on the mining frontier evolved through three distinct stages. The first stage came within a few weeks after an initial ore strike was made. Places were constructed overnight in the most haphazard manner, and in no particular order. The structures were made of canvas, logs or unseasoned lumber. Minimum cost and speed were the priorities.

The first saloon in town had to serve many needs in

addition to drinking and gambling; it might include a barbershop, bakery, dry goods store, etc. The place usually began in a tent; and if lumber were readily available, a rough shack would be built as soon as possible.

The booze served in these places was as rough as the surroundings. Usually raw alcohol was the base material. This was doctored with whatever ingredients the barkeeper found available.

One recipe, for example: "To one gallon of alcohol add five gallons of water, one pound of red pepper (to make it whiz as it runs down your throat), one pound of old government ovary tobacco to give it color and flavor, add two pounds of brown sugar; and I'll guarantee it to distribute as much happiness as anything an Indian can get hold of."

These concoctions were known as "forty-rod," because they could kill at a distance, or "chain lightning," "San Juan paralyzer," etc.

If the mining camp survived the first few weeks, the place began to take on a more permanent appearance. The small tents and crude shacks began to be replaced by more permanent structures. Thus began the second stage of the saloon development, the tents became larger, up to 100 feet in length; the shacks grew into wooden structures of logs or sawed wood. Some were a combination of canvas and wood. The better ones at this stage were frame construction, and had glass windows and wooden floors. The interior consisted of one room with a long bar, a few shelves, three or four chairs and portraits of Abraham Lincoln and General Grant on the walls.

Towns at this stage did not give an appearance of commitment to the long haul. They were in transition, and the population was ready to re-locate on short notice.

The transition of a town and its saloons to the third and final stage was gradual. The change encompassed both the structures in the town and its population. Prosperity attracted not just men, but men and their families. Business leaders appeared, law and order took hold, and streets were established in an orderly fashion. Places of drinking and amusement began to look more refined and permanent, just like the rest of the town.

One of the creative efforts associated with the western saloon was the "false front" seen in so many 20th century western movies. The purpose was to make the establishment look larger and more prestigious. Some false fronts gave the illusion of a second story with windows. Many were made of brick or metal to give the appearance a more "citified" look. The back lots of the major movie and television studios of Hollywood production companies had entire streets modeled after this special western architectural novelty.

Inside, the saloon improvements were everywhere. The interior was painted or papered, more tables and chairs appeared; and the bar itself became a permanent fixture of the building. Some entertainment equipment might include a piano, a billiard table or gambling apparatus.

In the larger, established towns, a really fancy, first rate saloon might be built from scratch, unlike most of the places that just evolved with a series of improvements over a couple of years. These new places could be quite impressive, and served to put the town "on the map." They were often two stories, and constructed of brick, stone, or California redwood.

Inside, the saloon could range from really first-class to overdone, ornate opulence. Paintings, French plate mirrors, chandeliers, fancy carved bars, upholstered chairs, glistening glassware and the all-important Brunswick pool table graced the larger places. Where women were available, the fancy saloons featured a bandstand and dance floor; gaming tables were in the rear.

The elite of the town were treated to special rooms only accessible by keys distributed to the chosen few. This was the western equivalent of the English private club.

Imagine all this in a town with plank sidewalks, mud streets and flimsy, mostly ramshackle buildings. The saloon was the town's showplace; its pride and joy, a credit to the town. It made one town superior to another.

In short, as the mining camp grew into a full-fledged community, its collection of saloons gradually came to resemble those of a typical American city. The bars began to reflect the economic, social and ethnic components of the town.

Within this diversity of drinking places ran a common thread—a customer entering any bar could expect certain sights and furnishings that defined the place as a bar, and were peculiar to the environment of a saloon.

Foremost was the bar itself, and usually the large mirror behind the bar. Artwork had certain common trademarks and the following pieces of art were almost always present in some form:

1. The sporting print featuring racehorses and/or prints of John L. Sullivan, the famous prizefighter; bare-chested and bare-knuckled.

2. Patriotism was always visible—portraits of the founding fathers; red, white and blue bunting; prints of "Custer's Last Fight" by F. Otto Becker were especially popular. Anheuser Busch distributed over 150,000 copies of Becker's painting; and it became a standard feature in both the West and the East.

3. But the most popular item of décor, which every saloon had to display, was the portrait of the naked lady. These damsels were voluptuous and posed in various stages of undress. Taken together this décor displayed an aura of masculinity, which makes sense since the clientele was almost 100% male.

One of the most favored items of an upscale saloon in the last half of the 19th century was the pool table. Pool had gained immense popularity throughout the country, and the arrival of the first pool table in a frontier town was a grand occasion. It was counted as another giant step along the path of civilization.

The popularity of pool/billiards increased following the development of composition cushion that provided more accuracy and uniformity. The primary manufacturer was the Brunswick Co., founded in Cincinnati by the Swiss immigrant John Brunswick.

It took awhile, but eventually even marble-bed tables made it to the West by wagons, riverboat and later, rail. All types were welcome, carom billiards, or four and six pocket. It was not too long before a bar was expected to have at least one table, and some had several. Well over a hundred years later, pool remains a popular form of bar entertainment. In fact, today, some bars are virtual pool halls with 20 or more tables.

The saloon proliferated in the western frontier to such an extent that, in many towns, drinking establishments frequently outnumbered all other businesses. The convergence of large numbers of ambitious, unmarried, male adventure-seekers on the western frontier created the kind of social disorder long celebrated in legend, and Hollywood and television movies. Barroom brawls, the reckless shooting of guns, and general drunkenness became commonplace. Alcohol-related deaths, often from exposure and ensuing pneumonia, contributed to the harsh realities of frontier life. Cold winters took a steady toll of the malnourished, chronically intoxicated unfortunates who failed to find their fortunes in the West.

Guidebooks promoted the prospect of finding immediate wealth to lure thousands of immigrants to California in the middle of the 19th century. As varying ethnic drinking customs were added to the melting pot, new and more explosive drinking styles emerged. The American frontier offered adventure, cheap spirits, and weak law enforcement; but it provided few leisure activities other than drinking.

Four factors seemed to have been influential in the development of the explosive drinking style that emerged on the western frontier. The first was the ready availability of cheap intoxicants. Because it was relatively easy to transport, whiskey was often the only beverage that could be hauled long distances over rugged terrain. In fact, frontier whiskey often consisted of pure alcohol mixed with water. By the early 1870s, technological improvements, which included bottling and pasteurization, led to the development of regional breweries such as Schlitz, Pabst, Blatz, and Budweiser; beer soon took its place beside whiskey as a favorite beverage across the West.

A second factor affecting the western drinking style was the character of the people attracted to the West. Men, who were unemployed, rootless and alienated, were particularly attracted to the frontier. This, in combination with their itinerant lifestyle, made the men develop drinking problems. These people were "drifters," fur trapping "mountain men," cowboys and miners. They lived hard, lonely lives, largely without families and without the social obligations or controls that constrained individual behavior back in the more populated East.

The third ingredient was the nature of labor and leisure on the frontier. Work on the trail and in the mines was long and monotonous, and drinking served as a relief from the drudgery. Thus the long continuous periods of work were broken by brief periods of intense drinking.

A final factor contributing to the development of the western drinking style was the lack of social controls on the frontier. Not only were there no constraints on the marketing and production of alcoholic beverages; but also there were not enough peace officers to control the lawbreakers. With the enactment of legal controls and the emergence of more stable communities, the western saloon eventually became more respectable, and so did its clientele.

The typical western saloon seen in Hollywood movies starring John Wayne, or on TV's hit show of the 1980s, Bonanza, came into being only after a community had settled down, when money began to flow, when the train came chugging into town. The moment was at hand when mahogany bars, gilded mirrors and white-shirted bartenders appeared and that depended upon location and development. In San Francisco, they appeared in the wake of the gold rush—early 1850s; in Denver, Colorado 10 years later; in Kansas cow towns shortly before 1870, in out-of-the-way places as late as the 1880s. Eventually the swinging doors and fancy mirrors were everywhere in the West.

The railroad in the 1880s brought the fancy, carved wooden bars to the West. Breen's in San Francisco has a 72-foot, straight, Brazilian, mahogany bar—supposedly the longest bar in America today. The record was Erickson's Saloon in Portland Oregon—684 feet long—over two football fields in length.

Towels always hung at intervals along the front of the bar for customers to wipe the beer foam from their beards and mustaches. A brass rail ran around the base of the bar to hook your boot heels over. Raising one foot helps your back when standing at the bar for long periods of time. Alongside the rail were the spittoons or cuspidors. The hardwood floor was covered in sawdust for easier cleaning. Behind the bar was the mantel, or back bar, built around a huge mirror. The back bar mirror was very popular because it doubled the apparent size of the room. It was also frequently the location of a favorite work of art—the nude female form. Lighting was by candles and kerosene lamps with some hanging from the ceiling. A central feature was always the pot-bellied stove.

Some of these saloons became famous, or infamous—Roy Bean, known as "the law west of the Pecos" held court in his own saloon, "The Jersey-Lily" in Langtry, Texas, a whistle stop on the Pecos River.

Gambling was big in the saloon—sometimes more important than drinking. Cards were the sport, Faro the game, and gold dust was the medium of exchange.

As you might expect with this all-male audience, saloon entertainment was "robust." Bull baiting, bear baiting and cockfighting were popular. As in earlier colonial times, hangings, sometimes multiple hangings, provided a full day of entertainment and drinking. Boxing and wrestling were also popular, bare-knuckled fights often lasted up to 100+ rounds, three minutes each.

Some of the entertainment was respectable, and lecturers were popular. Oscar Wilde was a drinker and lecturer on the mining town circuit: Leadville, Denver, Aspen, Butte and Helena.

The traveling fiddler was always a source of entertainment. Weddings were big occasions, but rare, due to the scarcity of women. Raucous or innocent, learned or illiterate,

89

cruel or genteel, depending upon time or locality; it all took place in the saloon.

Hurdy-gurdy houses were a western institution. The word comes from the name of the German instrument, similar to a barrel organ. Early saloons had a hurdy-gurdy man as the sole entertainment and the name stuck. These places had women in various roles to help push drinks—some were waitresses, others were dancers or prostitutes—sort of a version of geishas.

Honky-tonks originated in New Orleans and spread to the west coast. The girls danced with customers for fake drinks at outrageous prices. Not as lurid as today's "lap-dancing"; these dance-hall saloons were popular throughout the West.

The term "red-light district" supposedly originated in Dodge City from the railroaders custom of leaving their red brakeman's lantern outside the door of their girl of the evening to discourage intruders.

"Cat Houses" also originated in the West. When a Deadwood man discovered a fad among the "shady ladies" for cats as pets, he supplied them with cats for 25 cents apiece.

It is interesting that the huge popularity of state-run lotteries today parallel the popularity of saloon-sponsored lotteries in the 1860s. A customer in the bar might use a lottery to dispose of his revolver, horse, or gold watch. Sometimes a saloon-sponsored raffle might last a week or more; the excitement aided by the local newspaper giving a running account of the growth of the prize money.

One proprietor in Idaho offered his entire saloon, fixtures and all, to the winner of a two-dollar ticket.

THE SALOON OWNER

"The man behind the bar: When St. Peter sees him coming he will leave the gate ajar. For he knows he's had his hell on earth, has the man behind the bar." – Unknown

The saloon owner was typical of the men who patronized the bar in the West. He was a white male, usually single, and often an immigrant from most likely, Germany or Ireland.

One trait the saloonkeeper needed most was the ability to "hold his liquor." He was required to take part in every celebration, participate in every toast, and down his drink whenever someone bought a round for the house.

The barkeeper was also expected to maintain a proper balance between fun, entertainment, and freedom from social constraints; and peace and safety from the overly boisterous, obnoxious drunkard.

The bartender might accomplish this tricky balance using a number of approaches. A calming word might do the trick, or an offer of one last free drink. The owner would employ a technique of gradually escalating force on the tricky, belligerent offender. First, a few harsh words, then, perhaps a firm hand on the shoulder; finally, failing all else – he would provide a toss into the street. Keep in mind, that this had to be done while walking a fine line between acting firmly and forcefully, and overreacting, and using too much force on a relatively harmless drunk. This could result in the public rebuking the owner and a loss of business. In summary, he had to be a benevolent despot, acting reasonable at all times, while drinking consistently—if not constantly.

The saloonkeeper's public image was an extremely important ingredient for the success of his business. To this end it was necessary for the bar owner to remain visible to the public. He could accomplish this in a number of ways. Some became mayor of the town, or sheriff, or the sponsor of the drive for a new firehouse. All barkeepers were expected to give generously to the various town fundraisers.

The saloon owner usually cultivated a friendly relationship with the editor of the local newspaper. This was frequently done by supplying the editor with free drinks. In return the newspaper might run a column describing "happenings" at the bar, or the arrival of a new pool table, etc.

The saloonkeeper was often the most prestigious man in town. Dressed immaculately, just like the movies—white shirt, red vest, diamond ring, mustache, etc. He was part psychologist, impartial umpire of disputes, and great listener. The rule was discussions were limited to sex and sports—never politics or religion; still a good rule today.

Since the western bars stayed open 24 hours a day, seven days a week; another job of the bartender was to act as the town fire alarm—running down the street shooting his pistol to awaken the firemen when needed.

The western saloon served everything; much of it not really whiskey, just diluted, doctored, dyed, and flavored alcohol. The mainstays were rye, bourbon and corn whiskey. Bourbon was also known as "red likker."

The first brewery in San Francisco opened in 1837, in Denver in 1859. Beer was difficult to ship and breweries sprung up in every town in the West. Many bars served only beer—"beer gardens." The beer was stored in wooden barrels, and customers brought their own buckets, called growlers, to be filled with beer. Remember pure water, fit for drinking, was scarce.

Wine was also readily available. The Franciscan monks began producing wine in the southwest in the early 1600s.

Miners earned $3 a week in the early 1800s, and drinks were not cheap. Whiskey cost a quarter for two glasses; stand up to the bar and pour your own.

All saloons provided food, which almost always was meat only. In 1850 there were an estimated 50 million buffalo roaming the plains of the U.S. and no one grew vegetables.

The coming of the railroad changed the West in a very

short time. A variety of food finally became available. But it was the ability of large breweries to ship beer long distances that changed the western saloon. Louis Pasteur discovered how to kill bacteria by heating foods to 120°F, but then beer had to be kept cool at 70°F or less, or it spoiled. Anheuser-Busch established a line of icehouses along the railroad to the West to keep its beer cool. Then came the refrigerated railcar and Anheuser Busch had its own fleet of refrigerated railcars. Other inventions in the late 1800s helped the beer industry. A new keg tapping device was invented using carbonated gas to supply the pressure. Kegs could now be stored in the basement or under the bar; dispensing the beer did not rely on gravity.

In the 1880s, bottles were still blown by hand (mouth), and the top was made separately. By 1892, William Painter had founded Crown, Cork and Seal and changed the bottled beer industry with the "crown cap." Once bottles caught up with the technology, beer could be mass-produced.

The years from 1880 to 1900 were the "heyday" of the western saloon. The whole period only lasted 50 years, from about 1850 to 1900. For example, by 1880 Dodge City had 700 full-time residents, and supported "14 saloons and 47 whores." Cattle drives swelled the population. This ended when the railroad took over the job of transporting cattle from the West to stockyards in Omaha, Kansas City and Chicago.

In 1880, official records show 129 bar owners in Leadville, Colorado. The local paper claimed that 249 saloons had operated that year; apparently many owners had opened and closed in short periods. The population of Leadville was approximately 20,000. Regardless of these numbers and Leadville's fluctuating population, there was probably one saloon for every 100 people throughout the 1880s; and this figure includes women, children, and non-drinkers. Obviously the number of customers available to each barkeeper was small.

There were many reasons for the decline and fall of not just the western saloon, but saloons in general. Partially it was the fault of the saloonkeepers, the brewers and the distillers; partially it was the times, it was "chic" to be "anti-saloon." Also, bars in the West ceased to become a necessity—towns built churches, courthouses, meeting halls, and libraries that took over the functions once provided under one roof by the saloon.

The decadence of the saloon itself was a large cause of its downfall. The main problem was the immense spread of the saloons. The increase was due to beer not whiskey. The ever-increasing number of immigrants created a large appetite for beer. German brewers set up operations in every part of the country, especially in the West, and fierce competition was the result. The more beer produced, the more the saloons multiplied. By the 1870s the biggest brewers started to buy and lease the local saloons. Competition was intense and, they would spend a fortune bringing the place up to "grandeur."

The revival, once again, of the Prohibition or Temperance movement also contributed to the decline of the saloon. The old western saloon never came back—it had 50 glorious years, 1850-1900. So went the revolver, keno, poker chips, chorus girls, and the form divine behind the bar, the wall-length mirror, brass rails, spittoons, saw dust, red-vested, white-shirted, diamond studded saloonkeepers. The western saloon was replaced by bars, cocktail lounges, cafes, clubs, and "Ye-Old Taverns."

POST BELLUM YEARS 1865-1900

"Work is the curse of the drinking classes." – Oscar Wilde (1854-1900)

The Civil War caused great disruption in the drinking customs of this country. Rules were relaxed, laws not enforced, and the American saloon which already had begun to decline in quality, only became worse. Many unlicensed establishments appeared and their reputations were dubious. The temperance and prohibition movements practically disappeared, if only temporarily.

The period from around 1870 until the advent of Prohibition around 1920 is referred to historically as the "Saloon Period." Only in the U.S. was a common drinking establishment known by such a highfaluting title. By the time Prohibition was enacted, the temperance movement would make the word "saloon" such a "dirty word" that even when Prohibition was repealed, certain areas of the country forbade the use of the word in new bar titles. It became a synonym for a sleazy bar.

Following the Civil War many forces were at work to change the American drinking establishment. Industrialization was taking over, and men were required to work long hours at tedious and difficult jobs. Drinking on the job, long a custom (alcohol was even provided by many employers), was no longer allowed. It interfered with production, and the machinery made it dangerous. Drinking on the job was looked upon as both a moral and an occupational hazard.

Industrial work discipline affected far more than the conditions on the shop floor; and when workers had increased leisure time, and in some cases greater discretionary income, the saloon proved an inviting location for sharing the joys and frustrations of the job. Away from the employer's gaze, a bar

95

afforded some measure of privacy for workers who lived in densely populated urban neighborhoods.

Saloons opened as early as 5:30 A.M., and closed late at night, thus providing workers a location to socialize before and after work. In addition, patrons stopped in for the "free lunch" served by many establishments.

Beginning around 1870, the "saloon" period began to flourish. It was commonly known as "the poor man's club." The Anti-Saloon League called it "the devil's headquarters on earth."

Most saloons catered to a regular crowd (just as churches had their congregations), so most saloons had loyal constituencies of perhaps 50 to 60 "regulars" who kept them in business.

The principal appeal of the saloon lay in the opportunity it afforded ordinary working men to cultivate the sort of club life they found most enjoyable and useful during the industrializing years of 1860-1920. At a time when various groups, from Bible-thumping evangelists to profit hungry industrialists, were busy hatching schemes for re-shaping working class leisure habits, the saloon offered its predominately male clientele a place to work out their own solutions to their needs. There was a mesh between the market-oriented, profit-minded saloon enterprise, and the community or club-oriented values of the "regulars." The saloon satisfied the workingman's thirst for sociability, as well as his thirst for drink.

Transients relied on the saloon not only for food and drink, but also for sanitary facilities, warmth and, in some cases, a place to sleep for the night. Saloonkeepers cashed checks, received patron's mail, and provided free newspapers. Some of these services continued to be provided well into the middle of the 20th century.

Saloons offered the most common public setting for night time amusement, and they were located in every town—large or small. A very few establishments catered to the wealthy elite, but most affluent drinkers joined private clubs; consequently, the saloon tended to service working-class men.

In the smaller towns, evening entertainment was still limited to drinking, dancing and gambling. Urban areas provided large enough markets for entrepreneurs to offer ever-increasing entertainment choices.

Many of the amusements offered were popular primarily with the working class, and some often reflected ethnic preferences. Certain activities, such as sporting events, cockfights, gambling, and prizefighting, continued to be part of a male-dominated subculture centered on the saloon. This continues to this day with "sports bars" having satellite dishes to enable them to broadcast 16 different pro football games on a given autumn Sunday afternoon.

Men were well aware in the last half of the 19th century that their participation or enjoyment of these rough sports challenged the dominant, popular Victorian expectation that people would remain disciplined in work and in play. The very word "sport" implied social deviance.

Eventually those urban entertainment areas most associated with "sporting" activities became known as vice districts. Some became quite "famous": San Francisco's Barbary Coast; New York's Bowery; New Orleans's Storeyville (named after Alderman Storey, who sponsored the bill making the area a distinct vice district, including widespread prostitution). Following the custom that began on the frontier, prostitutes used red lanterns to signal their location; these neighborhoods were known as "red-light" districts. They were easy to locate since guidebooks for the cities included advertising for their services.

The term "skid row" originated in Seattle where Seattle's Skid Road was a track that was built to skid timber downhill to the sawmills. As Seattle grew, the area near Skid Road became a low-rent district of seedy bars, etc.

At that time, 1894, the Bowery section of New York City was just beginning to go to seed. It was declining as a theatrical street, but its saloons, dance halls, dime museums, gambling rooms, and brothels were still thriving. In that year, according to the police census, there were 89 drinking establishments on the

97

street that is only one mile long. On some of the side streets there were brothels in nearly every house—referred to as "free-and-easies."

As the 19th century progressed, sophisticated, mass-marketing strategies evolved to attract customers to the bars. Location, architecture, interior décor and music helped to set a nightclub or barroom apart from the drudgery of the working life. The activities of bars, clubs and dance halls were increasingly structured by the needs of the entrepreneurs, and by urban zoning restrictions. The saloon was a place to relax and be entertained. Since so many of the bars were neighborhood saloons, they helped to define immigrant ethics, and peer and gender cultures. There were Irish bars, very popular even today, German beer gardens, and bars that catered mainly to Italians.

Saloons helped immigrants find out about jobs in their new neighborhoods; and another advantage, the saloonkeeper might well speak the immigrants' native language. Since many bars were patronized almost exclusively by members of one ethnic group, the saloon became a cohesion-building social institution. Outsiders often received a chilly reception.

Patrons shaped a saloon culture within a context strongly influenced by brewers, distributors and saloonkeepers. By the late 1870s, competition among the many beer brewers was fierce. To keep their beer moving, the brewers began to buy the saloons or offer to furnish the saloon. In return, the saloon agreed to serve only one brand of beer. Vertical integration of production and distribution facilities helped the brewers maintain their share of the market as the number of bars continued to grow at a frenzied pace. At their height there were 500,000 retail outlets for beer and booze. The national average was one saloon for every 315 persons; this figure includes all people—women, children, etc.

Arithmetic began to work against the saloon owner. For example, if a town had 2,000 people and six saloons, about average, half the people were women, and 200 more were boys below the drinking age. Of the remaining 800 males, 400 did not drink—or drank only at home. That left only about 65 drinkers per bar. The bar owner had to hustle to get business. This did not endear him to the wives and families of the regular drinkers. Eventually the community might very well vote itself "dry."

The result was desperate competition among the bars, and conditions continued to deteriorate. The saloon owners were mortgaged to the hilt to the brewers and distillers so they would do anything to encourage drinking and make money. This included serving minors, mislabeling the drinks and cheating the customers.

Around 1880, competition began to become really rough. The big German breweries owned by families such as Pabst, Schlitz, Anheuser and Busch were now faced with large investments by British interests.

The cautious investors in England had a lot of idle money that they wanted to put into something safe that would earn around 6%. They wanted moderate income at minimum risk. The syndicate took over a string of American breweries at pretty fancy prices; it looked like a safe bet. Competition between the syndicate and the established beer barons became active. For awhile the breweries began to coddle the individual retailer and offer him a range of inducements to serve their brand exclusively. As the competition became more heated, the inducements increased from "free" advertising, to bar furnishings, to actually paying the rent. Then the beer barons and the syndicates began to open their own places. Saloons began to appear just about everywhere. Their sole responsibility was to keep the beer moving.

Pretty soon laws, rules, and good behavior all went by the wayside in pursuit of the dollar. Underage boys were permitted in the bar. Closing time meant nothing, "over-serving" the customer was common, as long as his money held out. Back rooms began to flourish with everything from gambling to prostitution. "Saloon" became a bad word.

An example of breaking the law resulted from the New York State legislature passing the Raines Law, designed to close all saloons on Sundays. Mr. William Raines worked out a very hard-boiled enactment, which provided awful punishment for any retailer who passed stuff over the bar on Sunday. However, as usual, the law had an "exception" in favor of hotels. Hotels were permitted to serve their guests on Sunday, provided the guests received their liquid nourishment with food properly set out on the table. So, guess what? Every saloon in New York City became a hotel. It set up a couple of cots, kept a fake register behind the bar, and the customers sat around a table with a "prop" sandwich on it. Everyone understood no one was allowed to touch the sandwich. They got away with it!

Some bars, joints really, had no glasses or cups. You simply sucked through a hose attached to a keg. One suck, three cents, for as long as you didn't take a breath. Take a breath and the hose was yanked from your mouth.

By the 1880s, three billion gallons of beer were being produced by the major licensed breweries. Between 1860 and 1900 beer consumption increased a staggering 40%!

Another custom aided the effort to increase consumption. "Treating, or "buy back," was the ritual of paying for a round of drinks for the "house," or at least for everyone at the bar. The bartender often initiated the first purchase; then everyone was more or less obligated to take his turn at buying a round of drinks. This, very often, as you can imagine, led to drunkenness and, as a result, legislation was passed forbidding it.

The "Treating" tradition has an extraordinarily long and venerable lineage. It was a feature of American colonial tavern life from the beginning, brought over by the English immigrants in the 1600s. They inherited their attitudes toward drink, reciprocity, and treating from distant Saxon ancestors of the 5th century, (or perhaps even from the remote cultures of ancient Egypt and Assyria). In antebellum America, the treating ritual thrived in worker's taverns, where it was customary for men to purchase half-pints of whiskey in turn to be passed around their drinking circle. By the beginning of the "saloon-period" in the 1870s, treating was already a centuries-old custom that constituted an integral part of barroom social interaction.

Treating was a complicated and delicate business. All episodes had an outward similarity. Men bought drinks for others in ritualistic fashion.

The first rule of barroom treating was, and remains, that the recipient was expected to reciprocate. Once you joined a circle of "treaters" you could not desert them. That would be the trick of a short sport, a quitter, and a cheat. It was part of the code of the bar that you had to treat back.

Most of the time the treat was purely and simply sociable—regulars buying drinks for each other. However, on many occasions the treating motivation could be more practical and self-interested.

There were many treating traditions that went beyond the normal buying each other a round of drinks. Often a customer treated when he had something to celebrate—the birth of a child, for example, which also called for a gift of cigars to everyone; a custom that continues to this very day, probably being wiped out by the ban on smoking.

A sudden windfall might prompt the buying of drinks—a new job and almost any good fortune. Even strangers could enter a barroom and wishing to celebrate, they would offer to buy drinks for the house. What a way to make instant friends!!

Many a business deal has been consummated in, or at the bar. The pleased participants would often include the bartender and other regulars in their celebration of sealing the deal.

Treating the barkeeper would seem like a peculiar custom. First of all, he could easily treat himself. Second, one of the cardinal rules for the bartenders was "no drinking on the job." The problem was for the bartender a treat was an offer he could not refuse. In order to stay sober, but not refuse any offered treats, the bartender often used a special glass called "a snit," which held an extremely small amount of beer, mostly foam. He was also permitted to accept a cigar in lieu of the drink with no offense to the "treater."

Often the bartender began the treating process by treating the house himself. This was usually employed when business was slow; and it obligated the customers to begin buying rounds of drinks.

The politicians' treat had a very visible purpose. In cities nationwide, the saloon was a principal arena of local politics, with the saloonkeeper serving as the main liaison and power broker between the machine politicians and the barroom voters. Pre-election treating went on year round; but on Election Day it reached a frenzied crescendo. Reformers, of course, considered this just one more black mark against the bar—bribing voters. However, you could view it as just a bid for mutual support and favor swapping, something that happened all the time. The regulars at the bar knew their part of the bargain—vote for the politician; no trickery was involved. This was a pact between the political leader and the constituent, and each would derive something of value from the arrangement.

There were, of course, some elements of society that used treating for immoral or illegal purposes. These types did not last very long in the typical workingman's saloon. They used drinks to improve their odds at cards or billiards; these were the professional gamblers.

There were prostitutes that hustled treats as part of their trade. For some sleazy bars this was an important source of income. The prostitute's job was to get the men to spend freely, encouraging them to treat the girls. Once again, both sides of the bargain knew what they were doing. Much of this behavior took place at "cabarets." The cabaret was an upscale bar that became prominent in the larger cities after 1910. These places featured live bands and dancing, and welcomed both male and female patrons. These were a sort of club, much like the workingman's saloon, and were soon labeled "night clubs."

Temperance advocates deplored the treating system, and its vulnerability to manipulation by self-interested parties. The saloonkeeper's treat, they felt, was designed to increase sales and increased drunkenness. The politician's treat was nothing more than a bribe for votes. The feeling of the temperance folks was that everyone had a motive for treating, and most of the time the motives were not good ones.

Thus, the saloon treat was many things to many people. To the reformers it was an abettor of extravagance, corruption, and drunkenness. To hustlers, it was a tool of the confidence game. To bartenders, it was a promoter of sales and goodwill. To politicians and sports celebrities, it was an instrument of public relations. But to most saloon-goers, those members of the "poor man's club," most of the time treating was a rite of comradeship that reaffirmed their status as regulars, and made a club of the drinking experience. What can be a more friendly gesture than buying a friend a drink?

THE FREE LUNCH

"My rule of life prescribed as an absolutely sacred rite smoking cigars, and also drinking alcohol before, after, and if need be, during meals, and in the intervals between them." – W. C. Fields

The idea of serving food in drinking establishments did not originate with the saloon period; but it was certainly carried to new heights with the introduction on a broad scale of the "free lunch."

The custom of serving food as well as liquid refreshment dates back to the monastic inns of the Middle Ages. The monks regarded it their Christian duty to provide hospitality to strangers on religious "pilgrimages." This practice was taken over as a commercial enterprise by English taverns in the 16th and 17th centuries. As we have seen, this tradition was brought to America; and colonial taverns were required to provide food, as well as drink and lodging. As America grew and people began to travel more, particularly by stagecoach, the demand for meals increased.

As noted earlier, the word "ordinary," used as a synonym for tavern, was derived from the term used to describe the public meal regularly provided around noon at inns and taverns in the South.

As America expanded and became more industrialized, with larger cities, and an expanding working-class population, the number of drinking establishments increased at a rapid rate. Soon, proprietors were searching for ways to attract a steady stream of customers. Many stories exist concerning the origination of the "free lunch." Some say it began in New Orleans; others suggested that a saloon-keeper-politician in Chicago introduced the "free lunch" by offering an oyster with every beer.

By the early 1880s the "free lunch" had spread coast to

coast; but when the major breweries became involved in the late 1880s and 1890s, the "free lunch" became a celebrated national institution.

As pointed out earlier, around this time the large breweries, many controlled by the British Syndicate, gained control of the urban saloons through direct ownership or exclusive distribution rights. In a highly competitive environment they were seeking a steady, regular customer base, just like the individual saloon proprietor. At the same time there was rising temperance sentiment against the saloon for its role in promoting public drunkenness. In retrospect offering free food was a great public relations maneuver on the part of the liquor industry. When temperance advocates began demanding that barrooms provide food to counteract the intoxicating effects of alcohol, the liquor industry responded by arranging to supply huge amounts of good, cheap food to all their saloons.

In a strange quirk of fate, the urban saloon now became the chief daytime source of sustenance for much of working-class America.

Furthermore, and even more remarkable, since any poor man who could purchase a five-cent beer could help himself to a decent meal, the saloons became the main food source for the poor and destitute. In Chicago, in the 1890s, it was reliably reported that all the charity organizations in the city fed fewer poor people than the saloons.

What a brilliant stroke the "free lunch" was for the big brewers. They were able simultaneously to satisfy the hunger of the working poor, and the demands of the nutrition minded reformers; all the while they were meeting their prime objective of establishing a steady, regular clientele.

And, as you might expect, this wonderful deal of a great lunch in exchange for spending five cents on a beer did not go unnoticed by the working women of America. The women normally used the side entrance, and sat in one of the back rooms; but very soon they also became regulars. Some young women received a weekly allowance for lunch; they commonly saved their allowances by eating the free lunch served in saloons. It is interesting to review a sampling of the food served at those urban saloons.   Though it was a nationwide phenomenon, regional and ethnic touches distinguished most saloon offerings.

Barrooms in the South, Midwest, and Far West generally offered more food than those in the East. This was due to higher food prices in the East, and the lower cost of liquor licenses in the rest of the country, which resulted in more saloons competing for steady customers.

Saloons in the West offered traditional country meals featuring hearty portions of beef and pork, along with bread and beans.   In the South, saloon lunches were really abundant. Describing a lunch in New Orleans, a customer could expect a long table with a tureen of soup, a platter of roast beef, baked beans and mashed potatoes.   Salads, bread, butter and sauces occupied another long table.   The fare was changed frequently, and due to the strong African-Creole population, included gumbo and chicken and seafood.

The lunches in the East were meager by comparison to New Orleans, San Francisco and Chicago. The lunch was usually cold, and consisted of bread, crackers, cheese, bologna, sausage, hard-boiled eggs, pickles and other relishes.

The ethnic make-up of the saloon's clientele had a significant impact on the food provided for the "free lunch." For example, one saloon in Chicago serving primarily Irish-Americans provided only potatoes. In contrast, a German saloon might provide sausage and a variety of pickled items, i.e., pig's feet, herring and ham. Bars in Catholic neighborhoods always provided fish on Fridays; since no meat on Fridays was a requirement of the Church through the first half of the 20th century.

Some of the fanciest places had the staff in uniform, and someone assigned to slice the beef, ham, or whatever, and pile it on the customer's plate. The Old Waldorf Bar opened in 1897 and lasted until Prohibition in 1920. This was "the place" in New York City at the turn of the century. Over a dozen white-coated bartenders were on duty at all times serving the thirsty needs of the country's major power brokers. The Waldorf, of course, had a "free lunch," but it consisted of caviar, Virginia ham, anchovies and canapés versus the normal pickled eggs and pretzels. Other places would only offer soup. Still others had a regular menu: Monday—hot dogs; Tuesday—roast pork; Wednesday—roast mutton; Thursday—Irish stew; Friday—always fish; Saturday— meat and potatoes. Lunch was not usually provided on Sundays.

The "free lunch" was normally stacked with items that encouraged thirst. Three of the most prominent were the pretzel, dried herring, and the sardel. The sardel deserves special mention. This limp, silver-coated minnow was a relative of the sardine. It was usually known by the German plural of the word, which was "sardellen." These creatures were soaked in brine, served whole, and left a taste in your mouth that caused a craving for another glass of beer. The sardel was more than a fish; it was a silent partner of the saloonkeeper.

To be fair, the typical "free lunch" was nothing to brag about. The idea was to set out as much cheap, thirst-provoking food as possible. It must be remembered for the average small saloon, the main idea was not to provide nourishment; the purpose was to sell beer.

Now there was a silent code of conduct that went along with the free lunch: you must purchase a drink. This was an unwritten rule and, in general, it was observed by the regular customers. No limit was placed on the amount a patron could eat, but common sense and good manners prevented over-indulgence at the food table.

Naturally, there were the moochers and deadbeats who seized an opportunity for a free meal. It was the barkeeper's job to keep an eye out for them, and throw them out if necessary. Some larger bars employed bouncers for this purpose. It should be noted that on many an occasion the saloon keeper would tolerate someone "down on his luck" and provide a truly "free lunch." This was especially true in hard times of strikes, plant closings and unemployment.

The strategy of the temperance reformers had really backfired. Requiring the saloons to provide food had led to the introduction of the "free lunch"; and the free lunch had introduced the saloon to a large group of people who never would have entered the place. Now, women and children were patronizing the saloon – the temptation was too great to resist.

Many aspects of the saloon "free lunch" were not good. First of all, the places were often dirty and unsanitary. Communal forks, for example, were rinsed in a glass of water in the center of the serving table and common-use towels, called mustache towels, were hung along the edge of the bar.

Newspaper reports and authors, known as "muckrakers," like author Sinclair Lewis, began to focus on the meat packing industry, and accused them of "routinely" doctoring spoiled meat with soda, and supplying it to the "free-lunch" saloon trade.

Times always change, and around 1900 the saloon keepers themselves began to become disenchanted with the free lunch. Many felt it was a lot of bother and expense for a few nickel beers. In the meantime, competition became stiffer from restaurants, company cafeterias, lunch wagons, and even from home cooked meals prepared by the increasing number of married workmen's wives. All the time the temperance movement continued to apply ever-increasing pressure on the entire saloon business.

Then, along came World War I in 1917, and the free lunch came under attack as a conspiracy between the large German brewers and the saloon keepers to undermine the food supply. The free lunch became unpatriotic.

So, the free lunch disappeared and has never returned. In the second half of the 20th century and up through today, it has been replaced by free snacks such as popcorn and pretzels and sometimes nuts.

The closest thing to the free lunch is the custom of serving hors d'oeuvres at cocktail time or during "happy hour." But this is not a workingman's lunch. The people of the saloon era depended on the free lunch for their main meal. There are some bars in major cities that do have elaborate spreads at five o'clock each day. The bar in the Ambassador East in Chicago, home of the famous Pump Room, served a bountiful spread of fruits, cheese, etc. every day. It often appeared that the thin, model-looking, attractive, young women purchased a glass of wine and had their dinner at tables near the bar. The bar didn't object because they were happy to have the attractive ladies present to attract the free-spending men.

DESCRIPTION OF THE BAR

"Always do sober what you said you would do drunk, that will teach you to keep your mouth shut."—Ernest Hemingway

The advent of the large brewers and the money from the English Syndicate caused a significant and somewhat standardized improvement in the interior appearances of the saloons. As the competition "heated-up," the furnishings of the bar constantly improved. Most saloons featured a hardwood bar of oak or mahogany that ran the length of the establishment. There was a narrow walkway behind the bar and behind that, built into the wall, was a back-bar consisting of shelves, cabinets, and a large mirror. The front of the bar had a brass foot rail, and frequently a handrail as well designed to accommodate the custom of stand-up drinking, so common during this period. Bar stools were rare, but tables and chairs were provided in the bar area. Huge brass cuspidors were placed at intervals along the floor, and sawdust was strewn about to absorb spills and prevent slipping. Murals featured prizefighters and reproductions of nubile, overweight nudes reclining on a couch; the favorites, nudes, were shaped like bass viols.

One popular description of the ideal girl of the time was one "you could span her waist with your two hands, but she couldn't sit down in a tub" – hope you get the picture!

The prizefighter pictures consisted mainly of John L. Sullivan. He was idolized as a man-killer and was a frequent saloon visitor himself—usually buying drinks for the house. This was long before he gave up the booze, and began to deliver temperance lectures.

Most saloons had a pool (billiard) table in the back room. Heat was supplied by a stove in the corner, and lighting was suspended from the ceiling (gas, and later electric). Toilet facilities were always in the back. Some establishments had a separate back room to be used by the ladies, or for meetings of organized groups.

Many saloons had a "ladies entrance" through a side door. This entrance had a three-fold purpose. First, it allowed women to come and go inconspicuously and avoid the scrutiny of reformers and neighbors. Second, the side door entrance eliminated the need to run the gauntlet through the length of the male-dominated barroom proper. At this time, the women were looking for sociability, not equality. Third, the side door provided easy access to the end of the bar where they could purchase "carry-out" alcohol. It also provided access to the backroom where women could attend social events, meetings, and feast on "free-lunches."

Music, especially singing, was always an important part of saloon life, and, of course, this led to establishments that specialized in music – "concert saloons." The major change in this area of the saloon business occurred just before WWI. Thomas Edison had invented the phonograph in 1877, and some "money-in-the-slot" machines appeared in bars at the turn of the century. It took until shortly before WWI for the recording techniques to be perfected enough to appeal to the broad market.

Following the War, the jukebox, along with the radio, pretty well replaced the individual or group belting out a typical 1890's Tin Pan Alley ballad.

The barkeeper of the saloon era had much in common with his previous heirs to the job throughout history. His appearance became more formal in the better urban bars, and his dress was almost like a uniform. He would wear a starched white coat with a geranium backed by a small fern in the lapel; he might have a bow tie or four-in-hand knot with a sparkling, solitaire diamond in the center. The bartender was always cleanly shaven and sported a moustache; his hair was usually well oiled.

As always, his job extended far beyond serving alcoholic drinks, and watching for free loaders at the free lunch table. Since alcohol has a way of transforming folks from meek and shy to believing they are tough and strong, the bartender was a frequent arbiter of potential fights. On the other hand, the really big tough guy might be changed into a weeping patsy by having a few too many. Others might suddenly assume they are the Caruso of the neighborhood, and burst into song. The bartender had to listen to all this. He was always a peacemaker, always a patient listener to the woes, grievances, and firm opinions of the customers. He had to be part bouncer, part psychiatrist, and part referee.

Alcohol is a powerful solvent and it has a way of removing the thin veneer of civilization. The Romans had a phrase, "In Vino Veritas," meaning "in wine there is truth." Sometimes, in fact quite often, whatever may be lurking in the mind of the drinker comes out. For a few people, depending upon the timing, this can lead to real problems. Once again, the bartender needed to be able to stay in control of his establishment; during all these moments he could never violate the cardinal rule of the bartender—no drinking on the job.

The bartender had two approved methods to avoid drinking on the job. The first— if the customer insisted that the saloonkeeper have a drink with him, he was to pour the drink into his private glass, called a "snit." The snit was kept under the bar and the interior was about the size of an eyecup. In addition, the drink poured into the snit was all foam. A good bartender could drink a hundred of these if necessary. The second method was for the barkeeper to accept a cigar in lieu of the drink. The old song was as follows: "I never drink behind the bar, but I will take a mild cigar." Both the drink and the cigar cost a nickel. A good bartender collected these all day, then put them back in the box and took a credit on the cash register.

The bartender, as usual, was an important man in the neighborhood. He usually had extremely good political connections; after all, the bar was the headquarters for local politics. He also was the man to see if you were in need of something or, worse, if you happened on hard times or trouble. Many a bartender could find you a job, a good lawyer, or give you a few bucks to "tide you over."

PARTIES AT THE SALOON

"I drink to make other people interesting." — *George Jean Nathan*

The bar, while serving as "the poor man's club," also served as his place to celebrate. This meant parties for everything from Catholic First Communions to Irish Wakes. Every holiday and feast day on the calendar was celebrated. Other places might close to observe a holiday, the bar stayed open to give its patrons a place to assemble and honor the anniversary or other occasion.

St. Patrick's Day was one of the high spots for saloon celebrations, especially if it was one of those spots where the bartender was known as Mike or Pat—not Otto!! In addition to the parades in all the major cities, the bars gave the Irish a chance to express their feelings for the British, and hope for the long awaited "Free Ireland." Even now, with the organized bitterness for England long dead, the custom of celebrating St. Patrick's Day in the bars of America stays alive and well.

Christmas time was an especially important occasion for saloon celebrating. During this period it was a tradition for the bar to provide a free "Tom and Jerry" for all the regulars. Now the saloon was always decorated to the gills with wreaths, holly and candles everywhere. In the center of all this was the huge "Tom and Jerry" bowl. It was a mixture of cream, sugar and beaten eggs. The key ingredient was usually rum, sometimes brandy; hot water was added and a touch of nutmeg sprinkled on top. A similar and popular concoction was eggnog; again, rum was the essential alcoholic ingredient.

It was natural that joyous occasions, such as weddings, were celebrated in saloons, but sad events were commemorated as well. It was a custom for the Irish to assemble in the neighborhood saloon after the wake. This usually led to a significant amount of drinking to honor the deceased. Other places might honor the death of a regular customer by placing a black crepe on the door of his favorite saloon.

The most familiar example of the era was the New Orleans jazz funeral. After assembling at a neighborhood saloon, mourners solemnly followed the hearse and marching band out to the cemetery for burial. Then they burst into a joyous dancing parade on their return to the barroom for a feast of food and drink to honor the departed.

Pieces of these customs are still honored today in the 21st century. The Church hall competes with the barroom for the place to serve refreshments to funeral service attendees; but the barroom continues to be the favorite for many people. After all, it's difficult to truly celebrate the death of the departed, or to drown your sorrows at this loss, without a drink. My wife and I were invited to an unusual celebration of life at our local bar in New Jersey several years ago. The setting was Briody's Irish Tavern in Rumson, New Jersey. One of the regulars at this bar, and there were many, including ourselves, was Jack Connelly. Jack was originally from Buffalo, New York, so that alone made us instant friends in a place like Rumson, New Jersey. We met at Briody's for over 20 years.

In December of 1996 Jack was diagnosed with terminal cancer and given six months to live. Jack had pretty good medical advice, including a niece and her husband who were medical doctors. With the diagnosis confirmed, Jack decided that no treatment was the best course for him. He never stopped his daily and nightly visits to Briody's till the very end.

In April of '97 Jack decided along with the help of his family, to have a farewell party at Briody's. So, they took over the restaurant and bar for a Saturday night party complete with band, food, "open bar," and dancing; people brought some pretty creative gifts. Invitations had been sent out well in advance. Like almost everyone else, we had never been to a party like this one; coming up with an idea for something to bring for Jack was not easy.

What a party!!! Jack, who at the time was only 62, still

looked fairly well—thin, but able to laugh and talk with everyone. It is especially notable that every single person that was invited managed to attend the party; they came from as far away as Florida, Chicago and Los Angeles. Nieces and nephews and other young friends were a special delight, since after several drinks they treated it like the party it was supposed to be— dancing, singing, drinking, joking, and celebrating Jack's colorful life. The party went on and on, well into the morning. I have several special thoughts I took away from that evening:

1. It was a great idea, and Jack Connelly had a wonderful time.

2. If invited, you must make a very special effort to attend—there are no second chances.

3. Try to bring a gift—it's difficult, but try. By the way, thanks to my wife Babs we had a poster framed which showed the facades of all the wonderful bars on Elmwood Avenue in Buffalo, New York in the '50s. Jack just loved it—memories for an Irishman of his home town.

Following Jack's death two months later, an empty glass was placed on the bar in front of his favorite bar stool, and no one sat there for a week.

One long-term American drinking custom disappeared during the saloon era. The longstanding "Saint Monday" tradition dates back to colonial days. Sometimes known as "Blue Monday," it was observed by some workers as their entitlement to skip work, or at least slow down, to nurse their hangovers, or perhaps indulge in a few more drinks to "sober up." Benjamin Franklin lamented in 1768 that "Saint Monday" is as duly kept by our working people as Sunday; the only difference being that instead of employing their time cheaply at church, they are wasting it expensively at the ale house.

"Saint Monday" was a casualty of the industrial age. Employers were not the only ones who would not tolerate absenteeism and drunkenness on the job; union leaders also argued that it undermined the cause of organized labor.

By 1900, the "Saint Monday" custom had disappeared and heavy drinking was confined to Saturday nights. Sunday drinking did not disappear; but workers had learned that they must separate their labor hours from their leisure hours.

PHOTOS

1. BRIODY'S – Rumson, New Jersey

2. PAT O'BRIEN'S – New Orleans, Louisiana. Pat O'Brien's claims it serves more alcohol than any other bar in the world.

3. FRAUNCES TAVERN – New York City. Famous Revolutionary War tavern.

4. 21 CLUB – New York City. Originally an upscale speakeasy; now one of the most famous bars in the world.

5. RALEIGH TAVERN – Williamsburg, Virginia.

6. BILLY BOB'S – Ft. Worth, Texas. Big, even by Texas standards. Holds over 6,000 customers and includes a rodeo arena.

7. P.J. CLARKE'S – New York City. Celebrity hangout for many years.

8. McSORLEY'S OLD ALE HOUSE – New York City. Open since 1854. Never closed during Prohibition

.

9. WESTERN SALOON – Colorado. 1880.

10. RAILROAD CLUB CAR - Delaware and Lackawanna
    Railroad. 1905.

11. NASSAU INN – Princeton, New Jersey. Founded in 1756.
    Famous Norman Rockwell mural behind the bar.

BRIODY'S – Rumson, New Jersey

PAT O'BRIEN'S – New Orleans, Louisiana.

FRAUNCES TAVERN – New York City.

21 CLUB – New York City.

RALEIGH TAVERN – Williamsburg, Virginia

BILLY BOB'S – Ft. Worth, Texas.

P.J. CLARKE'S – New York City.

McSORLEY'S OLD ALE HOUSE – New York City.

WESTERN SALOON – Colorado, 1880

RAILROAD CLUB CAR - Delaware and Lackawanna

Railroad. 1905.

NASSAU INN – Princeton, New Jersey

THE 'TAKE OUT' BUSINESS

"Sometimes too much to drink is barely enough" — *Mark Twain*

Irish immigrants arriving throughout the 19th century brought with them their long-standing custom of buying "take-out" beer from informal, home-based, grog shops known as "sheens." In Ireland these enterprises had constituted a thriving industry, often carried on by needy widows. It was an everyday pattern of immigrant Irish life as these places casually dispensed booze at all hours to friends and neighbors, men and women, for both on and off premises consumption.

This custom of taking a container (pail, bucket, can, etc.) to a beer source, having it filled, and returning home to enjoy it, became widespread throughout America. These generally unlicensed and unregulated home dispensaries survived in large numbers well into the 1880s. Gradually, however, the local governments began to force them to close in favor of the more easily regulated and more lucratively taxable, formally licensed, and brewery-backed saloons. The custom continued for decades; it was simply transferred from the home kitchen to the back door of the saloon.

So common was the practice around the turn of the century that in urban tenement districts the "take out" business far exceeded the amount of beer drunk in the saloon.

The custom eventually became known by the popular term "rushing the growler." It has been speculated that the peculiar term "growler" originated with the growling noise made by the can or bucket being slid along the top of the bar.

There were several reasons for the popularity of this "take-out" practice, but the primary one was the price. Saloonkeepers were by custom expected to charge no more than 10 cents for a "growler," regardless of the dimensions of the bucket, can, pitcher or other large container used to carry beer

125

home from the saloon. It is a little incredible, but this price of a dime for a growler lasted for over 50 years. Drinking anywhere near a similar amount inside the saloon would cost at least twice as much.

The "take-out" trade was deplored by the liquor industry because the profitability was almost non-existent. It was equally despised by the temperance movement for bringing on too much drunkenness, and for involving children, who were often used to "rush the growler" and bring the beer home to Mom and Dad.

Among working class folks, particularly immigrants from both Western and Eastern Europe, the custom was so entrenched that it was extremely difficult to stamp out. What finally made the growler obsolete was neither temperance nor profit, it was technology. In the early 20th century, bottled beer became available and along with it, home refrigeration.

In 1903, Michael Owens invented the first automatic bottle-making machine. Until then bottles were hand-blown and very expensive. Many were quite fancy and employed images of Benjamin Franklin or George Washington; some depicted a jockey on horseback or a Continental soldier. These bottles were the exception because of cost, and most booze was sold from a barrel and portioned into a jug.

PROHIBITION – ONCE AGAIN

"Alcohol is the anesthetic by which we endure the operation of life." – George Bernard Shaw

In the 1870s, a second wave of prohibition legislation began to sweep across the country amidst a growing concern over urbanization, immigration, and social disorder prevalent in almost every section of the country; alcoholic beverages and the urban saloon were singled out and given particular attention.

The Women's Christian Temperance Union was founded in Cleveland, Ohio in 1874, established by the Presbyterian Church. Frances Elizabeth Caroline Willard born in Churchville, New York, a Rochester suburb, was president of the WCTU from 1879 until her death in 1895. This woman was attractive and an excellent speaker. In addition to temperance, she fought for women's rights, suffrage, and civil rights. Five states adopted constitutional prohibition, while 15 states passed local option laws that allowed the voters in each town or city to vote for (wet) or against (dry) the sale of alcoholic beverages in their communities.

Eventually, municipalities began to regulate saloon growth by limiting the number of licenses issued, or restricting the number of hours the saloon could be open (no Sunday hours); or restricting activities, such as dancing. New suburbs sometimes incorporated as dry territories to set themselves apart from their wet metropolitan neighbors; thus emphasizing the continued association of the inner city with salacious nightlife. (This exists today in many forms. My family and I lived in three such areas during the '60s and '70s: Evanston, Illinois; Kingsport, Tennessee; and Little Silver, New Jersey. This movement against saloons was the old puritan dislike of everything that could come under the heading of pleasure—sex, gambling, acting, dancing, smoking and, of course, excessive drinking.)

Prohibition was a product of old-established Americans,

largely Anglo-Saxon Protestants, who resented and feared the behavior of the whisky, beer and wine guzzling new immigrants. Religious fervor took over and equated drunkenness with damnation, and temperance with salvation.

A book published in 1854, "Ten Nights in a Barroom," became the "Uncle Tom's Cabin" of the temperance movement. It was a smash hit for over 50 years and became a musical show. It described, in awful detail, death by alcohol of an entire town. In the second half of the 19th century, it was outsold only by "Uncle Tom's Cabin." Published with a picture on the cover of a little girl in a bar grasping her father's arm and pleading, "Father, come home," the book sold nearly 100,000 copies a year for twenty years. The play stayed on the stage for 50 years. The drunken father and the pleading daughter became such a well-known anti-saloon cliché, that it eventually became the object of parody in vaudeville skits.

President Rutherford Hayes' wife made the White House dry and became known as "Lemonade Lucy"; a common description of the White House, "where water flowed like champagne."

As this second great wave of prohibition began to fade during the period remembered as the "Gay Nineties," a new organization appeared: the "Anti-Saloon League of America." Their ultimate goal was to dry up the country bit by bit through local option laws and statewide prohibition.

The Anti-Saloon League was established in 1893 by the Reverend Dr. Howard Hope Russell at Oberlin College in Ohio. Working first with Methodist preachers, and then broadening to others, it became a national organization by 1895.

The man in charge of the national campaign was Wayne Wheeler whom Russell had found at Oberlin. He was a talented manipulator, had no real interest in Prohibition, and just wanted power. Wayne Wheeler was a political genius. The league pioneered pressure lobbying in Washington, and became the most feared and respected group of its day. As head of the ASL, Wheeler controlled six congresses and two presidents, and

CARRIE NATION

"The difference between a drunk and an alcoholic? Drunks don't have to go to meetings."—Unknown

Carrie Nation, born in 1846, a member of the WCTU, but really a one-woman force, set out on a mission to destroy every single bar in America (single-handedly, if necessary). Actually, she and her family were mental misfits—crazy!! She was six feet tall, 180 lbs., and her husband had died of acute alcohol poisoning.

She began a rage of wrecking saloons in Kansas using a hatchet. Kansas—where drinking flourished but Prohibition was the law. Ironically the law was helpless since she was destroying iillegal property. Alcohol wasn't the only thing Carrie Nation hated; others included sex, tobacco, and Teddy Roosevelt.

No movement was big enough to contain the formidable Carry Nation when, in 1899, tired of the pussyfooting tactics of the Temperance Union, she walked into a drugstore in Medicine Lodge, Kansas, with a sledgehammer and proceeded to smash a keg of whiskey to bits. The owner looked on openmouthed but, with dire results, did nothing. It was a political epiphany. She smashed, or as she put it, "hatchetized" her way through Kansas, engaging in acts of extraordinary violence, hurling billiard balls through saloon windows, first destroying casks of liquor and then, as nobody moved to stop her, reducing the furniture to splinters. Her evidently genuine destructive rages were so intimidating she was hardly ever challenged. When she did spend short periods in jail, she only emerged more determined than ever. She rapidly became a national media celebrity, smashing her way eastward through the bars of Missouri, Ohio, Philadelphia, and New York; publishing a ranting newsletter, "The Smasher's Mail," and turning herself first into an industry by selling autographed postcards and even miniature sledgehammers; and then a stage attraction in which she would act out her campaign on stage-set saloons, shrieking apoplectic poems amid the slivering glass. By now a hot property, she acquired an agent who was himself a drinker—a fact that seems not to have troubled her unduly—but her nemesis came when he booked her on a British tour. Londoners stayed away from her performances in droves, and when she tried to whip up interest by smashing a pub, she was arrested and fined. She was by now, of course, desperately unbalanced, but to her American audiences, the performances were a hoot.

In 1903, she turned up at a lavish New York ball hosted by Chuck Connors, an erstwhile boxer, bouncer, and low-life overlord who became one of the stars of the Bowery saloon scene. After sweeping bottles and glasses off the tables, and knocking cigars out of the mouths of bemused guests, she proceeded to read out a plea from a woman who had asked her to find her daughter. The crowd lobbed a bottle at her and Nation responded by pursuing everyone around the place with the famous hatchet. The whole venue erupted into a pandemonium of fistfights and shattered glass, until Connors himself did what hardly anybody had dared to do to her before, bodily throwing her out. All but disowned by the WCTU, she suffered a perhaps inevitable, complete, nervous collapse and died at age 65 in a mental institution in 1911. A few short years later her dream of a de-alcoholized America would come to official fruition.

late 1800s.

The following is a list of drinks with their alcohol content:
- Beer   5%
- Hard Cider   10%
- Wine   13-18%
- Distilled spirits   45% (90 proof)

Consumption rates for beer among persons aged 15 years and older rose from next to nothing in the 1830s to 6.4 gallons per year in the 1860s. After the Civil War the rate skyrocketed from 8.6 gallons in 1870 to 20.6 gallons in 1890, finally reaching a peak for the saloon period of 29.7 gallons in 1915.

Throughout the saloon era consumption of wine remained modest compared to beer and whiskey consumed by the Germans, Irish and Scots. Wine was consumed by Jewish and Italian immigrants from Southern and Eastern Europe. The per capita wine consumption rate for persons aged 15 and older ranged from only 0.6 gallons in 1900, 0.9 gallons in 1910, and dropping back to 0.7 gallons in 1915. This compared to 2 gallons of hard liquor and 20 to 29 gallons of beer per capita during the same period.

It is interesting that the "cocktail," or some form of mixed drinks, had been around since the early 1800s—but in the saloon culture, the cocktail was a "sissy" drink. If you needed a chaser with your whiskey, you were supposed to use beer.

Prices: around 1835, the standard price for a jug of whiskey was 25 cents per gallon, and the average customer received one shot of whiskey and a brass token good for another one of the same. Eventually the price went to 15 cents in the grand and swell bars, and stayed there until Prohibition.

The price had to include the revenue tax, government license, local license, rental of the establishment, contributions to political campaigns, and various church and social fund raisers, plus the free lunch and all the costs of general overhead.

The "saloon era" officially ended with the Volstead Act and national prohibition on January 16, 1920; but the patient began dying many years earlier. The actual causes of death were many.

One of the major causes was that there were simply too many bars. As competition between the large American breweries and the English Syndicate breweries became ever more intense, more and more bars were opened in the urban areas; the quality of the bars went in the opposite direction.

As the old-time saloon became more of an eyesore, the temperance movement had more ammunition, and the local voters began the process of wiping the saloon out. George Ade in "Old Time Saloon" describes his boyhood hometown with four saloons. "These four emporiums down by the rail station drew their entire trade from a total population of about 1600 counting all the farmers within a few miles. There were 16 other drinking places within a radius of 15 miles. Of the 1600 persons within our little zone, at least 1200 were women and children below drinking age; that left 400 men to support the four grog shops. Out of the 400 men, we can assume that about 160 never spent a red cent in a saloon—churchgoers, blue-ribboners, and others opposed to tippling. No saloon could count on more than about 60 dependable drinkers."

Mention was made of a college town with 20,000 population and 94 saloons; 1 saloon for every 212 residents. In the nearby villages there were more saloons. No kind of figuring can alter the fact that the average bar had a grand total of about 50 supporters.

The barkeep had to hustle to make a profit. He did the only thing he could do, and that was to encourage the spending proclivities of his own little group of "barflies." The "regulars" were roughly divided into two groups—those who dropped in, drank and departed, and those who kept hanging around and waiting for someone to come in and order all present to "belly up to the bar"; and there were those who just violently opposed going home early. There were others who contributed to the saloon; to the morning drinkers who needed a shot to get the day started, this was a necessity, not a celebration. Farmers dropped in for an afternoon beer and workers had a drink before going home, but all this was pretty sparse business except on Saturdays. This was giving the "hang-out" on the corner a bad name.

NOTE: At the turn of the century, there were fewer saloons in the 15 Southern states combined than in the city of Chicago.

In 1873 there were 4131 licensed breweries in the United States producing 9 million gallons of beer per year. By 1910 this had shrunk to 1568 breweries producing 53 million gallons per year.

From its rise in the 1870s to its demise in 1920, the saloon managed to serve the many needs of its working-class constituency remarkably well. Workers derived from the lore of the barroom a much-needed sense of shared heritage and common values. Drinking folkways, the free lunch, and the pastimes of storytelling, singing, and gaming helped the regulars find enjoyment and meaning in life. Further, the saloon provided an array of services and comforts which, for decades, were not readily available elsewhere. That a drink parlor should function

completely fell from grace. On the contrary, many men continued to regard it fondly as their personal club, and to patronize it to the end. But something had gone out of the old relationship when the saloon had stood at the center of everything happening in cities across the country. The secret of its success had always been to capitalize on the disorganized state of urban society in general, and the working class in particular.

Yet the confused and wide-open urban conditions that had sustained the saloon's immense popularity could not last. It was a great irony, in fact, that the saloon helped along the process of working-class self-organization that would be a major factor in its own undoing. By providing an arena where laborers could cultivate their common ties and develop solutions to their problems, it effectively hastened the day of its own demise at least in the form it had enjoyed in its glory days. Thus, the saloon was already slipping from its position of prominence in working-class culture when National Prohibition cut its history short on 16 January 1920.

WORLD WAR, PROHIBITION, AND 'THE ROARING 20s'

"Prohibition is better than no booze at all"—Will Rogers

As we have seen, temperance and prohibition had been around since Benjamin Rush introduced his "Moral and Physician's Thermometer" in 1784. From time to time they had gained momentum, as in the 1830s and '40s, and then faded with the Civil War and other priorities.

By the time of the beginning of the First World War, 1914 in Europe, and 1917 in America, the WCTU and the Anti Saloon League were poised to accomplish their mission to outlaw the drinking of alcoholic beverages in America.

Over eight million Germans had immigrated to the United States in the second half of the 19th century. Cincinnati was almost a German City—35% German, and over half the residents could speak German. There were 27 German newspapers and magazines in the Cincinnati area. Beer consumption in Cincinnati was four times the national average. There were 26 breweries and very little drunkenness. Germans tended to drink a lot, but did not seem to get drunk. Bob Newhart, comedian, has a great line, "I'm 25% German and 75% Irish—that makes me a meticulous drunk."

Milwaukee was, and still is, a very German-accented city, and Germans made Milwaukee famous. Beer has been synonymous with Milwaukee since 1844, when Jacob Best immigrated from Mattenheim, Germany, and opened the Empire Brewery.

America's entry into WWI on April 16, 1917 assured victory for the Anti Saloon League and passage of the 18th Amendment to the Constitution. A great wave of anti-German sentiment was sweeping the country. The ASL exploited the anti-German sentiment by reminding everyone that in America the breweries were largely German owned.

137

.

households began to experiment in their cellars or kitchens. A family could buy a still for $10, called "an alky cooker," and turn out several gallons a day. Local gangsters would pick the booze up for $2 a gallon.

The recipe was simple: mix the alcohol with 30-50% water, add a few drops of glycerin and juniper juice to simulate the flavor of gin. The bottles and jugs were too tall to fit under a kitchen sink tap, but they did fit under the bathtub faucet—hence the term "bathtub gin." The bootlegger or distributor got about $6 per gallon, and it was sold by the glass for about $40 per gallon.

The United States chemical industry was growing rapidly, and used 28 million gallons of alcohol annually. This was supposed to be rendered unfit for human consumption, "denatured," by adding some foul ingredients. In fact, however, much of the production was secretly directed to bootleggers.

Another area for illegal opportunities was the "near beer" industry. Near beer was made by first producing regular beer, and then removing the alcohol as the law required. As you might expect, not all the regular beer produced had the alcohol removed.

One unique way around the law involved "raisin cakes," which the Volstead Act permitted the vineyards of California to continue to produce so they didn't face total economic failure. Theoretically, the cakes were intended for the home production of sweet, nonalcoholic grape juice.

Demonstrators of the cakes, sales reps of the wine companies, cleverly told shoppers that "on no account should the jugs of juice be left in a warm place for 21 days because they might ferment and turn into wine; and don't put a stopper in the jug, because that would only aid the fermentation."

Beringer Vineyard in the Napa Valley of California, still in business today, was the trailblazer in exploiting the loophole. Other vineyards soon followed the lead.

This vast supply of illegal liquor was distributed to the millions of ready consumers by thousands of bootleggers. It was

wrist" penalty. Ninety percent of the cases were disposed of in a "bargain-day" manner. This is significant because the statute carried very tough penalties. Sort of like raising your prices when sales are poor, the department, admitting failure in 1925, increased the penalties for violations of the Volstead Act from two years imprisonment to five years; maximum fines increased from $1,000 to $10,000. General Lincoln C. Andrews, one of many administrators who attempted to direct the bureau during its troubled history, testified in 1925 that only about 5% of the liquor smuggled into the country was being stopped; only one out of every ten stills in operation was being shut down.

Two Prohibition Agents did their job well, and became famous at the time. Izzy Einstein and Moe Smith set the record for bars shutdown and booze confiscated over a five-year period in New York City. Their secret weapon was an unbelievable series of disguises. Izzy was a former postal clerk, five feet tall and 225 pounds. Moe, a cigar salesman, was slightly taller and even heavier. They entered speaks on Park Avenue in tuxedos, in Harlem in blackface, in sports bars as football players—ordered two drinks, showed their badges, and shut the place down. In 1925, they were fired "for the good of the service" according to the Prohibition Bureau. Others said the newspaper space they were drawing with their exploits was embarrassing to their superiors.

President Hoover called the 18th Amendment "a great social and economic experiment, noble in motive." Noble it may have been, but never has a law been more flagrantly violated. Officers of the law conspired with drinkers to make a travesty of Prohibition. Congressman Fiorello LaGuardia declared it would take a police force of 250,000 to enforce Prohibition in New York City; another 200,000 would be required to police the police.

In Texas, just a few months after the start of Prohibition, a still turning out 130 gallons of whiskey per day was found operating on the farm of Senator Morris Sheppard, one of the authors of the 18th Amendment.

An example of the magnitude of the enforcement task: in 1921 federal agents seized just under 96,000 stills and pieces of distilling equipment from bootleggers; in 1925 they took 173,000; in 1930 the seizures reached 282,000. And, this, of course, was just a small fraction of the stills in operation.

Winston Churchill arrived in California in the fall of 1929 on a speaking tour. Knowing the country was in a state of Prohibition, his son Randolph had packed a reserve of bottles of brandy, and other beverages.

A woman reporter upon Churchill's arrival in Seattle asked his opinion on Prohibition. Churchill replied by contrasting the British and American economies with regard to drinking. "We realize 100 million pounds a year from our liquor taxes," he said, "which amount I understand, you give to your bootleggers."

so their shops would not be harmed. Those who did not feel they needed protection soon found out when their trucks, stores, or even homes were burned or bombed.

The 13 years of Prohibition produced a criminal culture that has plagued America for generations.

While Al Capone was certainly "king" of the mobsters, George Remus, was "king" of the bootleggers. Remus was a Chicago lawyer; but when Prohibition arrived he moved to Cincinnati, and put his early training as a pharmacist to work. He purchased a dozen distilleries in Ohio, Kentucky and Missouri that the law had allowed to remain in business to produce medicinal alcohol. He organized an army of over 3,000 employees who distributed their alcohol from Chicago to New York City.

Remus lived a lavish lifestyle in a castle with a 125,000-gallon swimming pool; the common backyard pool holds about 10,000 gallons.

Following his bootlegging conviction, he went to the Atlanta penitentiary in a private rail car; when he left Cincinnati 500 admirers saw him off. At the penitentiary he took his meals at the chaplin's home, and had maid service and flowers for his cell daily. After 19 months in the pen, he came home to find his wife wanted a divorce—so he shot her. He was acquitted on grounds of temporary insanity; following the trial, he threw an elaborate party at the jailhouse for the 12 jurors. These were wild times in our history.

During Prohibition, prices of booze escalated. In 1930 cocktails went from 15 cents to 75 cents; beer was $10.50 per barrel in 1918, went to $160 per barrel; spirits rose from $1.39 a quart to $4.10 per quart.

Bootleggers openly distributed their price lists and even placed advertising in local papers.

In the 1890s, consumption of alcohol was made up of 45% spirits, 47% beer and 8% wine. By 1919, figures show consumption at 55% beer, 37% spirits and 8% wine.

During Prohibition, the mix changed to 75% whiskey, scotch, gin, and rum, and only 15% beer. This change was due to the poorer people, (the beer drinkers), not being able to afford the bootleg prices. The spirits, of course, consisted of everything imaginable, and the prices varied accordingly. The cocktail rose to prominence during Prohibition because it was needed to disguise the taste of the bathtub gin and other rotgut alcohol.

SPEAKEASIES

"I've had 18 straight whiskeys. I think that is a record." — *Last words spoken by the poet Dylan Thomas at the White Horse Tavern, New York City*

The term "speakeasy" came to describe the hundreds of thousands of illegal drinking establishments that sprung up like mushrooms following the enactment of the 18th Amendment. The origin of the word came from the custom of using a "password" to gain admission to the establishment.

In some areas of Chicago there were dozens of speakeasies per block. Al Capone controlled over 11,000 speakeasies in and around Chicago. In New York City there were 16,000 licensed bars before Prohibition. During the next 10 years, over 100,000 illegal speakeasies opened and closed.

In New York City in 1929, Police Commissioner Grover Whalen's men counted the speakeasies and came up with a nice round number, 32,000. But that was admittedly a low number; there was no way to count them. They existed in cellars in Greenwich Village, in penthouses off Park Avenue, basements in Manhattan—even in fashionable mansions and brownstones on New York's Upper West Side. There were 39 speakeasies on E. 52nd Street alone. They included hardware stores in Brooklyn, Wall Street office buildings—one on New York's Eastside had an exterior that made it look like a synagogue. There were thousands set up as soft drink parlors, restaurants or tearooms. In truth, they were everywhere.

Entrance to a speakeasy at the time could be a tricky thing. Usually it required an introduction by someone who had been there before. Then there was the business of registering the new patron's name, and perhaps issuing a special admittance card to be presented on future visits; many people had dozens of these cards. Doorbells had to be rung in a certain way, or a small sliding panel opened and you were "sized up," or the special

2,000 cases of wine is still shown to visitors today. A major raid by Prohibition agents in 1932 found nothing. During Prohibition it was known as "Jack and Charlies," for the owners' names—last name Kriendler. Two other New York "speaks" that continued in business long after Prohibition's repeal were McSorley's and the Stork Club. McSorley's saloon in Greenwich Village was so popular with police and politicians that it was never raided; it continues in business today.

Sherman Billingsley opened the Stork Club with money provided by gangster Frank Costello. We will visit this place in detail later, as it became famous in the '40s and '50s as New York City's #1 nightclub.

The Albatross in San Francisco was the hub of life in the Prohibition '30s. Renovated in the '70s, it stands now as San Francisco's first brewpub; here, a solid mahogany bar runs the full length of the building.

these items. A small painting of Old John done by a nearby Cooper Union College art teacher hangs on the wall back of the bar.

Another custom at McSorley's was no fixed closing time. When Old John, or later his son Bill, felt sleepy they would summon everyone to the bar and buy a round. When that was finished the place closed.

Thanks to the succession of owners, little has changed at the McSorley's Old Ale House today. It is a saloon from a hundred plus years ago.

The bar is short, accommodating only about five drinkers. It is on the right as you enter. On the left is a row of armchairs with their stiff backs against the wainscoting. Down the middle of the room is row of battered tables. In the center stands the old belly stove with its isinglass door; it is red-hot all winter. A painting of a golden corpulent nude stretched out on a couch playing with a parrot hangs right next to a portrait of Peter Cooper, founder of nearby Cooper Union College. Sawdust covers the plank floor. There are three big round dining-room tables in the back room. The kitchen is in one corner of the room. The food is simple; hamburgers, goulash, frankfurters, sauerkraut, potatoes and fried onions—that's it!!

The place opens at 8:00 A.M.; there is a free lunch of cheese and onions, and cold hard-boiled eggs are a nickel each.

The regulars start showing up by mid-morning. Most are from the neighborhood and come in every day. They are the "steadies," and mostly old Irishmen, many of these regulars stay all day. Some sit by the window and read the papers, some just stare into the street, some of which have brunch and doze off for an hour or two. Other clientele drift in and out: interns from Bellevue Hospital, students from Cooper Union College, garage mechanics, salesmen, and clerks from the many second-hand bookshops nearby.

By 6:00 P.M. the place fills up with working men from the neighborhood. Later the curiosity seekers arrive. They are merely tolerated, at best. Most tourists have learned about

McSorleys through the many paintings of the bar. Dozens of well-known paintings of McSorley's are scattered in museums around the country. McSorley's is probably the most painted bar in the United States. Between 1912 and 1930, John Sloan did five paintings which have become quite well known. One titled "McSorley's Saturday Night," was painted during the Depression, shows the owner Bill, John's son, passing out mugs of ale to a crowd of rollicking customers. McSorley's did not miss a day during the 13 years of Prohibition. Thanks to Tammany Hall politicians and local cops on the beat, McSorley's ran wide open, no peephole, no password, no payoffs or bribes; it was never raided. During Prohibition, McSorley's ale was produced in the basement in rows of barrels and wash sinks. A retired brewer would visit from the Bronx three times a week to make the brew.

Today, as since its founding, the ale at McSorley's comes from the Fidelio Brewery on First Avenue founded two years before the saloon. The brewery produces McSorley's Cream Stock and Old John's picture is on the label surrounded by the legend "As brewed for McSorley's Old Ale House."

The place has electricity, but the bar is illuminated with a pair of gas lamps. There is no cash register. Coins are dropped in soup bowls—one for nickels, one for dimes, one for quarters, one for halves and the bills are left in a rosewood cash box. The current slogan for the bar says, "We were here before you were born." It's still a tradition to urinate on the wall outside—men only!!!

for guests before dinner.

Officially, Prohibition lasted 13 years, 10 months and 18 days; December 5, 1933, the 21st Amendment was passed and repeal was official. It is worth noting that the 18th Amendment is the only amendment to the United States Constitution ever to be repealed.

When President Roosevelt proclaimed the repeal of Prohibition, he articulated the misgivings of many that the nation would return to its old ways of handling the liquor trade. He announced that the federal government would impose stringent codes on the production and sale of intoxicating beverages. He added "I ask especially that no State shall by law, or otherwise, authorize the return of the saloon, either in its old form, or in some modern guise." So, after 13 years of corruption, gangsters, bootlegging, and general lawlessness, it was odd that the saloon was singled out for special condemnation.

To prevent the large brewers to return to the custom of owning saloons, laws were passed forbidding them from owning beer outlets, or selling beer in any way, directly to the consumer. This created a huge network of beer and liquor distributors ("middlemen"), which exists to this day. This sales method was copied by the large soft-drink producers.

Beer was not popular during Prohibition since it was too bulky compared to liquor, which could be easily transported and concealed as required by the illegal activities of the time. The large brewers who continued to operate during the Prohibition years had to be creative. The Yuengling Brewery, Pottsville, Pennsylvania, used their refrigeration equipment to enter the ice cream business. By the end of Prohibition, Americans had lost their taste for beer; it was not until the 1970s that beer sales finally matched pre-Prohibition sales—over 50 years.

Perhaps no law in history did more for the cause of drinking than the Volstead Act. It introduced women to drinking for the first time on a grand scale; it was the source of the cocktail, the cover charge, and the speakeasy. But the most enduring legacy is the farce that the Volstead Act made of law enforcement. It left in this country a tolerance for crime and corruption at high levels of government and commerce. It remains entrenched to this day in the American psyche. Many speakeasies remained in business long after Prohibition's repeal as "after hours" drinking places. Organized crime remained strong for the next 70 years and is given credit for successfully establishing Las Vegas.

Many changes in America's drinking patterns took place following repeal of Prohibition.

Except for federal taxes, regulation of alcohol returned to the states that adopted a vast array of laws. Many of these stand in effect today. Examples include Pennsylvania, and many other states, which have state-controlled liquor stores. Some states adopted the monopoly, or control system, by which wholesale and retail operations were controlled by state governments. The remaining states regulated availability by the license system, which gave each state the power to grant manufacturers, wholesalers, and retailers the privilege of conducting business. Under both systems, the regulations were designed to prevent the abuse of the saloon era. Many localities in a vast number of states continue to prohibit the sale or serving of alcohol today. As of 2005, the nation continued to have over 500 "dry" counties. Another vestige of Prohibition, are the so-called "blue laws" that ban the sale of alcohol on Sundays.

A word about "blue laws." The term originated in Connecticut in the early 1700s where the rules forbidding drunkenness and excesses in dress on Sundays were printed on blue paper.

Historical note: George Washington heading to church was charged with violating a blue law in Connecticut that banned unnecessary riding or walking on Sundays—this was 1789. The 19th and 20th centuries expanded the blue laws to include bans on the sale of cigarettes, and included entertainment such as books, plays, and films. Today, 34 of the 50 states permit the sale of alcohol on Sunday. In the past four years, 13 states have added Sunday sales, mostly as a way to increase tax revenues.

South Carolina is an interesting example. Prior to 1973, South Carolina did not allow liquor to be sold by the drink. It was only available in state-owned liquor stores, which closed at sunset. People brought their own bottles into bars and restaurants and bought mixers and ice. Eventually it began to appear that patrons could drink an unlimited amount of alcohol and then attempt to drive home.

In 1972, voters approved a constitutional amendment to allow liquor sales by the drink in containers of two ounces or less. This was not unique at the time; several other states had similar laws. By 1990, Utah was the only other state to have a mini-bottle law; it ended the practice that year.

In an unusual set of events, the mini-bottle used in South Carolina wound up with the state having the strongest drinks in the country. Today, most bars and restaurants serve liquor in 1 to 1.25 ounce shots; sometimes 1.5 ounces is used.

Originally, back in the '70s, the mini bottle held 1.5 ounces. When the liquor industry went metric in the '80s, the bottle changed to 1.7 ounces. These mini-bottles are the same as the ones found on commercial airlines, and in hotel mini bars.

Several South Carolina groups, including Mothers Against Drunken Driving and the Baptist Convention, joined forces to have the legislature repeal the mini-bottle requirement. These groups felt the stronger drinks were contributing to more drunken driving. So, beginning in 2006, South Carolina bars and restaurants could use any size bottles they wish, and customers are getting a smaller drink.

BAR CARS

"I may be drunk, but in the morning I will be sober, and you, Madame, will still be ugly." — Winston Churchill's response to Lady Astor's accusation.

The golden age of the railroad bar car was about 1901 to 1933. The bar continued to exist, especially on commuter trains to New York City until the 1980s; but the decline of the opulent bar car on trans-continental trains began in the Depression years.

The gold standard for the bar car, officially known as the "club car," was established in 1902 on the New York Central "20th Century Limited" sleeper train that ran between New York City and Chicago.

These club cars were absolute marvels in every way—food, service and décor. The bar was carved mahogany, the fittings were solid brass, and the furniture was stuffed upholstery. The waiters' uniforms were immaculate—starched white jackets with contrasting slacks. Tables between the chairs held brass-reading lamps. The car even included a barbershop, shower, and smoking rooms. At every stop a news report, complete with up-to-date stock quotes, was provided to the club car clientele.

Since the bar car was predominately a male sanctuary, with plenty of cigar smoke, women and children rode in the "parlor" car, right behind the club car.

The railroads were highly competitive and used these famous trains as a form of prestigious advertising. In addition to the "20th century Limited," other outstanding trains of the time included the Santa Fe Chief and Super Chief and Burlington's Zephyr trains that traveled the West and Midwest. The Burlington introduced domed cars with swivel chairs for viewing the passing countryside while having a drink or two.

The wonderful service and magnificent surroundings cost the railroads a bundle, and all these famous trains lost money and were heavily subsidized by the railroads' freight business.

After World War II, the décor of the club cars changed

from the mahogany and brass look to a streamlined modern décor of stainless steel and fluorescent lights. Due to the increasing competition from the airlines for passenger revenue, the railroads gradually reduced the bar car service, and even the 20th Century Ltd. ceased service in the 1970s.

PRE-WORLD WAR II

"One more drink and I'll be under the host" — *Dorothy Parker, Algonquin Hotel Round Table Group*

The end of Prohibition brought another "beginning" to the American drinking establishment. Gone was the wonderful neighborhood, ethnic saloon, even the word saloon was now considered "bad taste." The term cocktail lounge, or just lounge, replaced "saloon," along with clubs and cafes. Since no new bars had been built in the U.S. in the 13 years of Prohibition, a flurry of construction took place, and the bar architecture was decidedly "modern" for the times. Nightclubs, which had begun to flourish illegally during Prohibition, were an instant hit in all the major cities. Dancing was extremely popular; and the cocktail once invented to disguise the awful taste of bootleg alcohol, expanded its flavors following repeal of the 18th Amendment. Lots of other changes followed Prohibition's repeal. There were 3500 breweries before Prohibition and 400 remained after Prohibition, and 200 of these closed during the '30s Depression. The introduction of the metal beer can by Adolph Coors in 1935 aided drinking at home; beer was previously available only in returnable bottles, or on tap in the bar. The non-returnable bottle became available much later.

Hotels and restaurants now blossomed with bars, cocktail lounges and taprooms. These were modern places with fancy equipment.

Following Prohibition, the bars' customer base also changed. During Prohibition drinking became quite expensive, and as a result it was the province of the middle and upper classes. This broadened the base beyond the former poor and downtrodden. After Prohibition the price of drinking in general dropped substantially, but liquor remained expensive due to the high government taxes. As a result, beer once more returned to popularity. Beer was not taxed at the same rates as liquor.

In an odd twist of events, the illegal manufacture,

distribution and sale of alcohol continued on a major scale following repeal. Part of this was due to the huge taxes levied by the states and the federal government on legal booze. Liquor continued to be smuggled into the country and illegal moonshine stills continued to operate, especially in the South.

Even with Repeal over, one-third of the states imposed their own prohibition laws. Eight states continued to ban the sale of alcohol, other than what was called "3.2 beer", a weak beer containing 3.2% alcohol. Fifteen states, primarily in the South, forbid the sale of liquor "by the drink," and eliminated the sale of alcohol in bars, lounges, and taverns. Counties and smaller towns continued to remain deeply divided on the subject of Repeal. Over one-half of the states made the retail sale of liquor and wine a state monopoly. These state-controlled liquor stores operate in many states today; Pennsylvania, and South Carolina, for example. Some new laws prohibited "perpendicular drinking" to thwart the return of the dreaded saloon. This meant you had to be seated to drink, no standing at the bar with your foot on the rail. Utah today has a law forbidding anyone to have more than one drink in front of them at a time; underage drinkers are not allowed within three feet of the bar.

After Prohibition, the big brewers never went back into the business of owning saloons. The connection had hurt them badly, and they were not about to repeat the mistake. In addition, they were prevented from owning bars by federal law.

The big drinking news of the '30s was the expansion of the nightclub establishment in major cities—especially New York. Many of these clubs started operating in Prohibition days. The Stork Club for example was opened as a speakeasy on New York's West 58th Street during Prohibition; it later moved to East 53rd.

As the '30s progressed the national economic depression following the stock market crash of 1929 began to affect everything and everyone, including the booze business. This put a lid on the expensive nightclub business until prosperity returned with the beginning of the Second World War.

The Great Depression dislocated a lot of people and their families. A great migration occurred with Southerners moving across the Southwest and the West. They brought with them a rural institution, the "honky-tonk" saloon. These small joints were usually located on the outskirts of town, and country and western music with dancing was the featured entertainment. Hundreds and hundreds of country-western melodies memorialized the honky-tonk bar and more importantly, the "honky-tonk" atmosphere. Sad songs—the wife's gone, the dog died, the car won't start, the job disappeared, etc.!! Guitar was the music, and it grew louder with acoustic and electric instruments. Some of these places grew into nightclubs with Western and frontier themes.

The state of Nevada legalized gambling in 1931. Gambling and brothels were common throughout the mining and logging towns of the West. Nevada made it legal with the hope that it would attract capital and people in the midst of the Depression. It certainly worked, although much of the capital came from organized crime—another result of the Prohibition years. Today it is all legit and to categorize it as successful would be a gross understatement. Las Vegas is now planning to open a museum dedicated to displaying the role of organized crime in the early success of the gambling resort.

Meanwhile the workingman's bar, maybe not the wonderful saloons of pre-Prohibition, but still a "watering hole" for a poor guy, returned in force.

Walking two blocks to Public School # 2 in Olean, New York from 1937 to 1946, I had to pass two pretty "tough" drinking establishments; if I walked two more blocks past the school, I would have passed two more. This was on a commercial street called State Street containing typical small town shops; i.e. hardware store, drugstore, soda fountain, and radio repair. By any count, this city of about 20,000 at the time, must have had at least 50 neighborhood drinking establishments. These were local bars, located on commercial streets adjacent to solidly residential neighborhoods. One of the two bars I passed, four times a day by the way, since we came home for lunch, was named "The Cabin." The motif, such as it was, had a bit of a log cabin appearance. The doors were always open on decent days. I can still recall the odor on warm days—unpleasant, pungent, stale beer. A large, really large, St. Bernard usually slept on the top step at the entrance. Since everyone felt it was necessary to give the poor dog a taste of beer, it is no wonder he slept all the time.

Just as back in early colonial tavern days, the place had two entrances; one opened directly into the bar, the other opened into an area filled with tables and chairs. It was here that the establishment met the New York State requirement that drinking places had to serve food. From the appearance of this place, a large number of regular patrons must have been poisoned on a frequent basis. The dining area had a stage and a dance floor where a small band took over on Friday and Saturday evenings. The surprising fact is that this scene was repeated all over Olean, every day and night of the week during a time of great poverty and stress. The names of some of these places give a glimpse of the time, The Silver Slipper, The Wheel, Dinty Moore's, The Brown Bear, Red Garter, Clancy's, Welch's Bar, Capitol Hill, and Wayne Street Tavern.

There was a vast array of other places to imbibe as well. Every conceivable fraternal order was represented and served alcohol—The Moose, Elks, Knights of Columbus (Catholics), Christopher Columbus Lodge (Italian), Pulaski Club (Polish), Veterans of Foreign Wars (VFW), American Legion, Hibernian Club (Irish). In addition, there was the City Club for the local professionals, and the Bartlett Country Club for the golfers and upper class. Every place had a full liquor license.

As in most industrial cities, some of these bars in Olean were located close to a factory's entrance gate. This was where people had a beer or two on the way home from work. Sometimes they dropped in for lunch, and the whole family might drop by for spaghetti or meatloaf on a Saturday night, and always a fish fry on Fridays. Just as in the "saloon days," the bartender knew everyone; he most often was also the owner. He would cash your check, lend you $10, help you locate a plumber, electrician, whatever!   It was here that you socialized with friends, neighbors and fellow workers, and kept up-to-date with what was happening on the local scene.

This make-up of drinking places has endured till today with some changes of course—but many of the clubs still operate; the seedy bars continue to exist—some in the same locations as in 1938.

WORLD WAR II

"Always remember, I have taken more out of alcohol than alcohol has taken out of me."—Winston Churchill

The United States entered World War II on December 7, 1941. It affected the American bar scene through a shortage of booze, of young men, and of bar workers. These were counterbalanced by an abundance of money, and people seeking entertainment in a very tense time in our history.

Sugar rationing eventually put the moonshiners out of business. Liquor shortages resulted in a black market, as shortages usually do. Twelve-year-old scotch whiskey, for example, was in high demand. Prices of all alcoholic drinks went up. The government placed a 20% tax on amusements, calling it a "cabaret tax"; it was later increased to 30%. This caused the nightclub business to decline significantly, and the government was forced to repeal it.

Help was so difficult to find that the 21 Club in New York City posted a sign, "Be kind to the waiters, we can get all the customers we want."

Although booze was not rationed during the war, it became very scarce along with numerous other items. Whiskey all but disappeared in 1944 as increased wartime thirsts drank up the five-year stock that distillers were supposed to have on hand before they converted totally to industrial production. The distillers were permitted to direct one month to whiskey production in August 1944. Whiskey distilled from potatoes became popular.

Canned beer disappeared because of the tin shortage, and saloons frequently ran out of beer. Hijackers and racketeers seized the moment to begin filling empty cans and bottles with watered-down beer and booze.

Liquor stores kept the good stuff back for regular, old customers, and even these folks had to pay black-market prices, and were often forced to buy several bottles of just awful stuff in order to purchase one bottle of real whisky. Once again, just as in Prohibition years, terrible concoctions were put on the market, some containing methol alcohol resulting in blindness and death.

It's an interesting sidelight to note that the three leaders of the allies during WWII were all pretty good "drinkers."

Harry Truman, president from 1946 until 1952, awoke each day at 5 A.M. and began the day with a shot of Old Grand Dad bourbon and a glass of orange juice. He commented, "It got the juices flowing." Truman, an avid recreational poker player, had an active bar with two U.S. Navy bartenders on duty in the poker room of the "Little White House" in Key West, Florida. This location served as the functioning White House of the U.S. for almost six months of Truman's presidency.

Winston Churchill, certainly the leading citizen of the world in his time, was generally recognized as a smoker of fine cigars and a drinker of true magnitude. This genius of a man lived life with joy and gusto—to the fullest. Of course, no one could consume the amounts of alcohol for which he is often given credit. Some of this is due to the fact that he was a "slow drinker" and appeared to always have a glass in his hand. However, a look at a typical day—seven days a week, illustrates a significant amount of alcohol intake.

He usually had a drink brought to him an hour or so after breakfast. This whiskey and soda would last until lunch. At lunch he drank freely of champagne, port and brandy. After lunch, about four, he would order another whiskey and soda that would last until time for his nap. Dinner was a repetition of lunch, and he would call for his first drink in the evening around 10 or 11, depending upon when dinner finished. He would probably have a second or third whiskey before retiring for the night, probably around 1, 2, or 3 A.M. Keep in mind that it was during these early morning hours at the end of a day of continuous drinking that Churchill dictated most of his famous literary works.

Here are a few other points about this man who is often credited with saving Western Civilization by opposing Hitler and the Nazis at a most critical time, 1939-41. Churchill did not drink cocktails. During his three-month stay at the White House during World War II, FDR mixed martinis every evening at 5 P.M.— Churchill rarely participated. Another unusual characteristic, Winston Churchill never poured his own drink. He always called for his valet and said "A whiskey and soda, please." At lunch and dinner however, he did pour the champagne and the port wine.

Dinner would begin with a bottle of champagne placed in front of Churchill. He would pour for everyone within reach and then pass the bottle around for others to help themselves. The port was for dessert and went well with the Stilton cheese, Churchill's favorite. Brandy and cigar time followed dessert. This could last from one to two hours at lunch and dinner. At some dinner parties, five or six guests would frequently finish a bottle of brandy before leaving the table.

One more final story concerns Churchill's first stay at the White House during World War II's earliest days, December 1941.

Churchill summoned Roosevelt's butler, Alongo Fields, and issued the following directions which he termed "orders": "First, Fields, I don't like talking outside my quarters. Second, I hate whistling in the corridors. Third, I must have a tumbler of sherry in my room before breakfast, a couple of glasses of scotch and soda before lunch, and French champagne and 90-year-old brandy before I go to sleep at night." It should be noted that of his many biographers none ever described Winston Churchill as having difficulty sleeping.

One of the beneficiaries of WWII was the rum industry, the business that had been replaced 150 years earlier by the whiskey enterprise. Now with distilleries forced to produce industrial alcohol for the war effort, it wasn't long before whisky supplies began to disappear. Since rum was produced in the nearby Caribbean, it was both cheap and available. Sales of rum increased three-fold during the war and the dance bands played a new hit song "Rum and Coca Cola."

The bars in towns across America continued to serve the needs of workers who were putting in long days; the end of the work day still required a drink and a little conversation, and weekends were still used for a family treat. With the extreme gasoline shortage and strict rationing, the population was forced to patronize establishments close to home, usually within walking distance.

Dancing was extremely popular during the war years and this made bars with juke boxes, or ones with live entertainment on the weekends, popular. Adult nightclubs, after a slump at the beginning of WWII, resumed the boom they had enjoyed prior to 1941. Prosperity enabled the famous New York City clubs to set revenue records every year of the War. Big city nightclubs began raking in enormous sums due to the wartime economy. One week, with Jimmy Durante as the headliner, the Copacabana in New York City took in $62,500. Keep in mind an Army Private earned $21 a month. Places like the Copacabana, Latin Quarter, Billy Rose's Diamond Horseshoe and the Zanzibar were grossing $40,000 to $50,000 per week. This trend was nationwide, and the bar business throughout the country was up 40% over 1941 to $250 million annually. All this occurred despite food and gas rationing, a liquor and beer shortage and a 20% Federal amusement tax. Prices also went up, and a drink cost $1.25 each. Really scarce items, like 12-year-old Scotch and 15- to 18-year-old rye or bourbon, developed thriving black markets.

All these posh clubs had entertainers who went on to Hollywood and became big names into the '50s and '60s. Frank Sinatra played at the Wedgewood Room of the Waldorf Astoria; the Persian Room belonged to Hildegarde, the Chanteuse from Milwaukee; at the Copa it was Joe E. Lewis and Jimmy Durante. Stars like Perry Como, Dick Haymes and Dean Martin were featured at other spots. Other clubs featured dancers, jugglers, magicians, and—whatever would draw the crowd. Some places, like the Stork Club, Toots Shors, Lindy's, and Jack Dempseys, people went just to see each other and the celebrities who might

171

be there.

Some of these clubs had long lines outside every night, and only the folks selected by the doorman gained the right to enter and spend their money. Another difficulty for the bar and nightclub business was the practice of wartime curfews. Early in 1945, the government ordered a midnight curfew for all nightclubs, theaters and other places of entertainment. The idea was to save fuel, manpower, and transportation. Workers were upset, especially swing shift workers, who got off work at midnight and sought a little relaxation thereafter.

New York Mayor LaGuardia, who was up for reelection that year, citing the large group of servicemen who could be deprived of their valuable leave-time, advanced the curfew to 1 A.M. The Army retaliated by sending Military Police to clear the bars at midnight. As you might expect, after-hours clubs and speakeasies returned to New York.

When the midnight curfew was imposed in New York City, Toots Shor, whose restaurant bore his name, made the famous remark: "Any schmuck ought to be able to get drunk by midnight." Toots Shor's was a highly popular nightclub in New York City into the '50s and '60s. The bar's proprietor and namesake was a stocky Jewish boy who toiled his way up from busboy to bouncer, to owner of one of New York's most celebrated nightspots. He was a rags-to-riches, hard drinking, American success story.

The rich and the famous gathered there every night, notably Jackie Gleason. "The Great One" parlayed his legendary drinking ability and wonderful comedy skills into becoming the number one entertainer on U.S. television during the late '50s and '60s, and into the '70s, with a show called the "Honeymooners."

Gleason and his drinking buddies Humphrey Bogart, Frank Sinatra, Milton Berle and others hung out at Toots Shor's. Gleason went so far as to have a replica of Toots Shor's bar constructed on the movie set of "Papa's Delicate Condition" to be used as his dressing room during the filming of the movie.

Dancing and nightclubs rose in popularity on the home

172

front. Some of the more famous ones in New York City exist till this day. Others closed when times changed in the '60s and '70s. Some well-known spots that have closed include Lindy's, Dempsey's, Toots Shor's, and the Stork Club, and recently the Rainbow Room at Rockefeller Center.

In May 1945, one count put the number of nightclubs in New York City at 1100, or one-third of the nation's total. The number of patron visits per year at 2.5 million—this was an increase of five times over 1939.

All of these places were known as "society cafes"; they were aggressively promoted by the newspaper gossip columnists of the city. There were 14 daily newspapers in New York City with featured columnists such as Dorothy Kilgallen of the Journal-American, Leonard Lyons, and Walter Winchell who had a popular radio show. Ed Sullivan had a column in the Daily News that he parlayed into a hit TV Show, "Toast of the Town." These people spent their evenings visiting these nightspots and gathering material for their daily columns. No wonder Dorothy Kilgallen died of an overdose of alcohol and drugs.

The Stork Club began as a "speakeasy" on West 58th Street in Manhattan. Sherman Billingsley became famous as the proprietor of the Stork Club. He had quite a background, even served prison time at the Federal penitentiary in Ft. Leavenworth, Kansas on a Michigan bootlegging conviction. When the legitimate Stork Club opened on East 53rd Street, it was financed with organized crime money from the Costello Mafia family. Not an unusual arrangement in those days.

During and following WWII, the Stork Club became the place to be seen. Sherman Billingsley didn't have customers; you were considered Sherman's guests. Walter Winchell had his special table there every night, and he promoted the club constantly in his columns and radio broadcasts. The Stork Club welcomed an average of 2500 patrons a night. It became so famous that WWII bombers were emblazoned with the Stork Club emblem—a top-hatted stork.

In 1945, a movie titled "The Stork Club" debuted,

featuring stars Barry Fitzgerald, Barbara Hutton and Robert Benchley, and based on life at the club. The club even had a TV show beginning in 1950 with Sherman Billingsley interviewing celebrities at Stork Club tables.

The Stork Club thrived during and after WWII; but the changes in social custom in the sixties finally forced it to close in October 1965. There were too many confrontations with labor unions that brought years of picketing the premises. Some still trace the decline to the day John Kennedy was shot—Jack and Jackie were frequent and long-time Stork patrons. It was never the same after that.

Sherman Billingsley, bootlegger and nightclub owner extraordinaire, was in the club every single evening, and he never drank hard liquor. He died October 1966 at age 70, and the Stork Club became a public park.

1950s

"My mother is over 90, still doesn't need glasses, drinks right out of the bottle.—Henny Youngman

By 1950 I was 17 years old. Winters in Olean, New York were cold and snowy—and they still are cold and snowy. The legal drinking age in New York State in 1950 was 18. During WWII the draft age was lowered to 18, and the thinking at the time was "if you are old enough to go to war, you are old enough to drink." For some reason the drinking age has been raised to 21, but you can still go to war at 18!

Different groups of teenagers in different parts of town hung out at their own bars —ones that accepted a younger crowd as long as behavior was acceptable. For example, at our place, "The Wheel Restaurant and Bar," located right in our neighborhood, we were restricted to the table and chair or "dining" section of the restaurant. Just like Colonial times, bars continued to have two entrances, and we were not permitted in the bar.

Money, of course, was limited and beer cost about a quarter, so it was important to make a bottle last a long time. Unlike teenagers today, economic circumstances usually prevented any one of us from having too much to drink. We would spend a typical couple of hours in the "Wheel" either shooting pool, or more likely playing shuffleboard. This was not the electronic shuffleboard of later years. The shuffleboard hardwood table was about 20 feet long and 30 inches wide. The object was to slide a weighted two-inch diameter disk the length of the board and stop at a designated scoring space. A team consisted of two players, with one represented at each end of the table. A disc that hung partially over the edge of the playing surface scored extra points. The opponent could attempt to knock your disc aside by hitting it in turn with his disc; pretty much the same as outdoor shuffleboard played on a larger surface with larger discs propelled by using long-handled sticks.

Hours were spent in the bar talking, drinking a little, and playing shuffleboard. Some of the group became very expert at this pastime. It should be noted that this underage drinking was confined to boys; no girls participated. Other bars in the early '50s had pinball machines or darts. This was just before the introduction of television to America and the local tavern.

A typical small town usually had at least one drinking establishment with live entertainment for listening and dancing. In Olean it was "The Capitol"—its arrangement had the bar and barstools located just inside the entrance. Beyond the bar were arranged 15 or 20 tables of four chairs each. A dance floor and a small bandstand were at the very back of the place. This was a place to meet and entertain girls. Naturally, it took more money to "hang out" at "The Capitol" than at "The Wheel."

Other bars in town were similar and attracted their own clientele: older or rougher or wealthier. One bar located on Union Street, Olean's main thoroughfare, had carved out a unique niche over the years since Prohibition. "Welch's" offered the opportunity to eat, drink, and gamble. Placing an off-track bet on the horses was illegal at the time—but readily available if you knew where to go.

Other bars in this town of 20,000 ranked at the low end of the scale by any measurement. Places like "The Brown Bear," "Dinty Moore's," and "The Cabin," were dark, dingy, dirty and smelled of stale beer. They opened early in the day and, as far as I could tell, never closed.

The acceptance of illegal bars during Prohibition spawned another type of drinking establishment after Prohibition—the "after hours" club. These places were everywhere in America and in Olean it was known as "Jack Hoard's," after the name of the owner. This place looked like a cabin, and was located in woods about seven or eight miles out of town. Those folks who hadn't had enough to drink by "last call," usually 1:00 A.M., could then drive the seven or eight miles to Jack Hoard's place and drink as long as they could afford it.

Places serving drinks illegally existed in every part of the country. "After-hours" could mean different things in different places. Some counties, and even entire states, permitted no drinking on Sundays. Some bars in larger cities were allowed to stay open until 2:00 or even 4:00 A.M. using a "nightclub license."

Living in Kingsport, Tennessee, a town of about 35,000 in northeast Tennessee in the late 1960s, we had no bars. Drinking was only allowed in private clubs, and you had to furnish your own booze. This, of course, led to much excess, since you were pouring your own drinks without regard to measuring the amount. In addition, we had to go to neighboring Virginia to purchase the booze, since the sale of liquor, beer or wine was not permitted in Kingsport, or Sullivan County. To make matters more complex, the closest state controlled liquor store in Gate City, Virginia was not permitted to sell wine; that required a separate trip to a state store in Abingdon, Virginia which sold only wine.

So in Kingsport, and many other places, especially in the South, during the 1970s, drinking alcohol required membership in a club, i.e., Elks, Moose, VFW, local country clubs, etc. The club had a place to drink, so-called grill or barroom, but no booze; you had to furnish your own. The illegal activity that the local law-enforcement was concerned about was the slot machines all these clubs operated. They were usually raided every four years when the local sheriff was up for re-election.

Traveling to Dallas, Texas in the early '60s and staying downtown at the Baker or Adolphus hotels, I had a locker behind the bar with my bottle in it. They at least had a bar and a bartender to serve the drinks from your personal supply.

In the Midwest there were private "clubs," usually located beyond the city limits, known as "roadhouses." A member could bring as many guests as he wished, and the roadhouse furnished the alcohol.

Leaving Olean, New York to attend Purdue University in

West Lafayette, Indiana in 1951, I was 18 years old and used to drinking beer legally. I was shocked to learn the legal drinking age was 21 in Indiana. And let me tell you, at least in this college town, the law was strictly enforced. Even having alcohol in your own dorm room could get you expelled from school. This, of course, did not mean that no one under 21 drank booze or beer. There will always be ways to get around the rules, and there were certainly lots of parties with lots of drinking.

The only bar located in West Lafayette, Indiana in the 1950s was known as "Harry's Chocolate Shop," and this monopoly on drinking extended into the 1970s. The authorities there seemed possessed with making sure only legal drinking took place, and only at one establishment. However, it is worth noting that Lafayette, Indiana, a short walk across a bridge over the Wabash River, contained many openly promoted whorehouses, in addition to a collection of bars. One of the more notable parlors was located upstairs over an auto repair shop, named "Quick Service." The brothel was appropriately known as "Quick Service Mary's," using the name of the proprietor.

The prevailing opinion at the time was that these brothels were needed as an outlet for the predominately male university specializing in engineering and agriculture. There are probably no available records to indicate whether grade averages improved or fell, or whether campus rapes increased or not, following the close of these establishments in the late '50s.

College bars have been part of the American landscape since the founding of William and Mary in Williamsburg, Virginia in 1693. Records indicate the students socialized extensively at the taverns located within a short walk of the school in colonial days.

Founded at Yale University in 1909, the "Whiffenpoofs" are the oldest a cappella singing group in the U.S. (famous for "The Whiffenpoof Song"). The group of 14 senior men still tours the world each summer. During the school year they perform on Monday nights at Morey's Temple Bar near the Yale campus, where they have been singing for 100 years.

Many evenings in the '50s, my future wife and I would go to Cole's Bar on Elmwood Avenue in Buffalo, New York. This was a wonderful college bar and typical of the era. The walls were covered with college pennants from everywhere in the USA. It featured a 50-foot long bar with lots of bartenders and a mezzanine with tables for those who wanted a little more quiet. On the main floor, with the jukebox playing, it was usually packed. It was the place to be. Cole's is still there, and much is the same—pennants on the walls, terrific bar and lots of young people from Buffalo State University and the surrounding area. I'm sure everyone reading this section recalls their favorite college bar, and all the wonderful memories the place evokes.

The local, neighborhood bars were thriving during the 1950s, and some are still doing well today. A typical American neighborhood bar was Ted Finewood's "Ship" located on busy Dewey Avenue in Rochester, New York. This was a workingman's bar surrounded by a middle-class neighborhood of houses built in the '20s and '30s. It was located within walking distance of Kodak Park, a mammoth industrial complex employing over 25,000 people at the time.

I had just graduated from college and began working at Kodak in August, 1955. The Ship, was a short walk from a boarding house where I had rented a room for $28 a month. I would visit the Ship on a very regular basis. An illuminated sign hung over the sidewalk, "The Ship." The front windows had neon signs promoting the two local competing beers—Genesee Beer and Standard Ale; each of these brands had a large brewery located along the Genesee River in Rochester. This typical bar had the traditional two entrances. The one on the right opened into the bar, and the one on the left led into the "dining area." The place smelled like beer—not like food.

This was a wonderful place on a cold, snowy, winter evening. Early in the week, Monday through Wednesday, the place would be practically empty. Many establishments paid their employees on Thursday or Fridays, and as a result, business picked up dramatically on the weekends. The bar had a television, a new addition in the '50s, usually playing one of the popular quiz shows – "$64,000 Question," until the cheating scandal involving the piano genius Van Cliburn ended the show. An electronic bowling machine was located at the far end of the bar. For a quarter you could attempt to knock the pins down by sliding a puck or disc about six feet. It was nowhere near as much fun as the old shuffleboard game; but again, newer and much more efficient. You could sit at that bar and strike up a conversation with a complete stranger. Beer was 20 cents and Ted Finewood wouldn't bother you if you bought just one and stayed at the bar till closing.

The dining side contained nothing but a jukebox—five tunes for a quarter, and about a dozen tables with four chairs each; clean as a whistle and no customers until Friday nights. A fire ended the business in the 1970s.

The industrial Midwest and Northeast were filled with these neighborhood bars. An article in a June 2000 issue of the Rochester, New York newspaper described the closing of Jack Ryan's Bar that had operated for 67 years, since 1933, at 1650 Lake Avenue across the street from Kodak Park.

The current owners had operated the place for 40 years. Jack Ryan's was typical Formica table tops, pin ball machine, pop corn machine, pool table, a couple of neon beer signs in the windows. This bar was located on a busy strip center along Lake Avenue that had a barber shop, White Tower Restaurant, a small department store, etc. The main entrance to Kodak Park was located across the street, and the streets and avenues behind the bar contained middle-class housing for Kodak employees who walked to work. These folks were the patrons of Jack Ryan's bar.

The bar closed permanently 10 years ago and the contents were auctioned off. As the owners for the past 40 years put it, "a neighborhood bar requires a neighborhood." Parking lots have replaced the houses. As for Kodak, things have changed there too, not for the better. At shift changes, thousands of workers would be coming and going and many would stop at Jack Ryan's for a beer on the way home. This was a gathering spot, but not anymore. There are many fewer workers, working longer shifts. When work is over they hop in their car in one of those parking lots and drive to the suburbs.

The owners lived right around the corner from the bar; the children all worked at the bar before going on to college and successful careers of their own. People would come in for a beer, a hamburger, a cup of coffee and some conversation. The owners knew everyone; cashed their weekly paychecks, went to the kid's weddings and the grandparents' funerals. Times change, workers don't want to be seen going into a bar for lunch anymore.

1960s – 1970s

"Never mistake endurance for hospitality" – Unknown Bartender

One of the most popular bars in New York City during the '60s and '70s was Mike Manuchi's, named for the owner, a former boxer.

The bar was oval, and sports photos and paintings covered the walls. Sports figures and celebrities frequented the place; and it was a hangout for the advertising crowd (noted for its expense accounts and heavy drinking.) The bartenders were just ideal for this type of place, knowledgeable about sports, friendly, and poured a big drink.

One evening a friend of mine stayed a little too late. Just prior to "closing," about 1:00 A.M., he decided to use the bathroom; which was located in the basement. George proceeded to fall asleep in one of the stalls. Somehow the person charged with making a final "sweep" of the restaurant failed to notice him. Well, of course, when George finally woke up in the basement the place was closed, dark and deserted. What a surprise when he opened the bathroom door to find his way upstairs to the exit; George came face to face with a snarling, growling Doberman Pincher on night guard duty. No choice for George but to spend the remainder of the night in the restroom. The last straw came when the morning kitchen help arrived and he tried to leave the bathroom once more. None of the help spoke English, and seeing a stranger in the place at 7:00 A.M.,— they called the cops.

This was 30 years ago. I saw George recently and he told me once again "never had a single alcoholic drink since that night!"

Two other true stories involving friends of mine occurred about this same time in New York City.

The Kitty Hawk Bar near Grand Central Station, in addition to having an aviation motif, had a very, very, large bay window facing the street. One evening a friend of mine was giving an ad hoc demonstration of a military drill-team maneuver known as "spin arms." A golf umbrella was substituting for the normal rifle. Well, Ron gave that golf umbrella a great spin, and somehow it left his grasp and landed point first in the middle of that bay window. Nothing happened for the first few moments; and then that entire window looked like a spider's web. You can only imagine the cost of replacing a window of this size in the center of Manhattan.

The other story demonstrates a popular myth of the times, "that the good Lord took special care looking after drunks." After a special celebration at the Algonquin Hotel on 44th Street in mid-town Manhattan, my dear friend proceeded to walk right through the glass front door – without opening it! Glass everywhere, not a scratch on Jim.

The Biltmore Hotel in New York City located near Grand Central Railroad terminal acted almost like a Club in the '50s and '60s. A huge clock graced the lobby, and the standing tradition was to meet someone "under the clock" at the Biltmore at a specified time. The place would be jammed with commuters after work, having a drink and checking the clock for the departure times of their trains leaving Grand Central Terminal for Connecticut. Meeting a date before or after Ivy League football games, Yale vs. Harvard, "under the clock" and retiring to the Palm Court for drinks was part of New York society.

As described earlier, at this time women were not allowed in the Grill Room of the Biltmore. If an unsuspecting female did enter the bar accidentally, everyone would begin to whistle and boo until she left, which was usually immediately. This changed with the women's rights movement of the '70s, and the Biltmore fell to the wrecker's ball in 1981.

A mind-boggling culture change took place in America between the calm of the early 1960s and 1970. The early '60s included young people wearing bobbed hairstyles, saddle shoes, penny loafers and crew cuts for the boys, and pleated skirts for the girls. Evening entertainment meant a ride in the car, a movie, followed by a hamburger. By the end of the decade this had changed to long hair, beads, and psychedelic clothing.

The '60s were tumultuous times for young Americans. The long, drawn out Vietnam War inspired a counter-culture in this country, which eventually opposed and attacked all traditions. "Don't trust anyone over 30" became their motto. In addition to the War, these movements embraced civil rights, women's lib, and environmental concerns. Drugs entered the American scene in a major way during the '60s. Beginning with marijuana and spreading to LSD, heroin, and cocaine. Some called it "the turn-on, tune-in, dropout" decade. Today there is a popular saying, "If you remember the '60s, you weren't there."

Alcohol played its part as well. Between 1960 and 1975, the annual U.S. consumption of alcohol increased by one-third— two gallons per capita by 1975—still only half as high as in 1830. In the late '70s, consumption of alcohol reached 2.82 gallons per capita, ranked 15th in the world, ahead of Ireland and Sweden, but below Germany and Canada.

This was a result, in part, of teenagers drinking earlier and in larger numbers. In addition, the drinking level of women approached that of men. Year 1978 was the peak for the consumption of hard liquor; then a decline set in that extended till the end of the century. A lot of this decline was caused by a national switch to wine and beer.

Speaking of beer, the first low calorie, "lite" beer was introduced in 1961 by Trommer Red Letter Beer. And, the first tab beer cans arrived in July, 1963.

Now, we must say that all the drugs, protests, "love-ins," and Rock-'n' Roll bands, did not change the typical bar scene for most adult Americans; but, it changed it "big time" for young Americans.

Most small and mid-size towns continued to thrive with neighborhood bars, much as in the '40s and '50s. In large cities, clubs and cabarets featured jazz by Louie Armstrong, Miles Davis, Dizzy Gillespie, etc. Dave Brubeck played at Kelly's; a wonderful small cabaret in Chicago; and in New York City, West

52nd Street was a haven of bars and clubs featuring avant-garde jazz.

Meanwhile, the young people were developing a subculture featuring drugs instead of alcohol, and music that drove older folks crazy. Clubs catering to this group sprung up in every major city. The renowned ones were located in the Haight-Ashbury part of San Francisco, and in Greenwich Village and the East Village of New York City.

Specialized bars served college students, conventioneers in large hotels, and tourists at major attractions; other establishments catered especially to gays and lesbians, one of the few public places homosexuals could socialize. Bars were opened in airports, museums, even in laundromats.

A landmark in the gay rights movement occurred in June 1969 when working-class gay youths finally resisted a punitive raid by the New York City police at the "Stonewall" bar in New York City. Once again, a bar played a major role in the history of this country. The resulting publicity ended harassment of gays by the New York City police department.

Beginning in the '60s, national and regional chains of bars and bar-and-restaurant establishments developed throughout the country. These have spread and can be recognized by their typical décor: an oval bar, important for encouraging conversation; as opposed to the traditional bar, which the bartender stood behind, and the customers were forced to stare at the wall, the mirror, or count the bottles on the rear shelf. It did not foster customer friendliness and verbal exchange. These new style bars are known today as Fridays, Ruby Tuesdays, and Applebee's. Others like Olive Garden, Red Lobster, and Outback have bars, but the emphasis is on food. These places are on top of the current national fad for food and drink. It may be Mexican food and a variety of Margarita drinks, or perhaps Buffalo spicy chicken wings and beer, or cheese-and-wine bars. In major cities, bars are opening and serving only wine or martinis.

In the freewheeling days of the '60s, and women's liberation promoted with much vigor, a woman named Carol

Doda caused a sensation at the Condor Club in San Francisco. She performed a dance, called the "Swim," topless. To say this lady was buxom or well-endowed hardly described the enormity of her breasts. This was the beginning of the topless bars and nightclubs; and the fad spread from California to the rest of the country and remains an active part of the bar scene today. The names vary from "topless" to "adult" bars; but the features are the same. Dark, dingy, cheap booze, open every hour of the day or night. Attractive, usually, ladies dancing on a stage or on the bar in the skimpiest attire permitted by the local law enforcement department. At the Off Broadway and The Cellar restaurants in San Francisco, the waitresses wore only bikini underpants and high-heeled shoes. In the 70s, several North Beach bars featured topless shoe shines for $20.

One other special bar did not have the same staying power. In the early '60s, Ray Zembryki was Vice President of Iroquois Beer in Buffalo, New York. Buffalo had once had over 30 breweries, this was down to eight by 1947, and by 1964 there were only two—Iroquois and the William Simon Brewery. The television ads of the big brewers like Budweiser, Miller and Schlitz touted their products as premium beers, and this appealed to the young people; the result was fewer sales for the local outlets.

Zembrycki came up with the idea for the mobile bar. It was a refrigerated truck holding kegs of beer with taps for the beer on the side. It was really a walk-in cooler on wheels. The vehicle became an instant success, and was first used at the Erie County Fair. For a while, it and many others like it, made appearances at every major outdoor event that permitted sale of alcoholic beverages. For the record, Iroquois founded in 1820, by Jared Roos, a Dutch brew master, went out of business in 1971.

The "Bier Bike" has become a fixture in Cologne, Germany. It is a strange contraption, about the length of a stretch limo, mounted on four rubber tires, with a giant keg of local beer mounted in front. Behind the beer keg sits the jovial driver dressed in his alpine hat. On either side there are two, long, bar tops, six seats on each side, and one at the rear presided over by a bartender. There is no motor! The vehicle is propelled by the patrons who climb up on their seats, order a beer, put their feet into the bicycle stirrups and begin peddling. After they have had enough beer or exercise, they give their seat to the next customer. The Bier Bike follows a regular route through the city, and it is a highlight of the annual Oktoberfest event.

The first singles bar supposedly opened in Washington, D.C. in 1965, and was described by women as a meat market; women sitting around were being stared at like pork chops on a plate. Only nothing was for sale, they were all giving it away. This new found freedom to display the female body in bars and clubs found its way into Playboy, a racy magazine for the times; it led to establishing a chain of clubs throughout the country. The first Playboy Club was opened in February, 1960 and these places became a big hit in the '60s and '70s. They were designed to look like mansions from the late 1800s. The staff was entirely female and consisted of "showgirl" quality waitresses in attire that amply exposed their legs and breasts. In order to gain admittance to the Club you had to be a member; that required payment of annual dues. For the dues you were given a key; hence the name key clubs. The Playboy "hostesses" had costumes designed to affect a Playboy bunny look, which was the Club's logo—rabbit ears and a fluffy white bun for a tail. Men could sit around in very pleasant surroundings drinking and smoking, and ogling the girls. They even had an authentic poolroom where you could challenge one of the hostesses to a game. You seldom won, she was usually an expert player; but the men enjoyed watching her bend over the table to line up a shot.

The Playboy organization expanded this Club concept into full-scale resorts in suburban areas close to large cities. For example, one was located at a ski resort in Great Gorge, Mt. Vernon, northern New Jersey and close to New York; and another on Lake Geneva, Wisconsin, between Milwaukee and

Chicago. Women were not barred from these clubs, and occasionally accompanied men just for the experience; but, of course, almost all the customers were male.

The concept was so popular it spawned copycats in all the major markets. One very successful one was known as "The Gaslight Club." As the name implied the interior resembled a gas lit saloon from the San Francisco gold rush days. These bars were rarely outlets for local beers, and usually offered national brands that featured mass-marketed promotions. It may be Super Bowl Sunday, St. Patrick's Day or the Fourth of July. At its height, there were 22 Playboy Clubs and one million key holders. Of course, like all fads, these clubs lost their cachet and disappeared in the '80s. Now, two decades later, the Playboy Club is attempting a comeback in Las Vegas. No membership key will be required; just a cover charge gains admittance. Plans call for opening at least10 more around the world.

By the 1970s, discotheques and nightclubs were created in styles to accommodate the varied tastes of the customers. For example, disco music in the '70s and rap music in the '80s swept the urban clubs. Prestigious clubs in New York City and Los Angeles employed doormen or bouncers to screen patrons for appearance and dress deemed appropriate for the particular club's culture. The lucky entrants considered themselves important and privileged to gain entrance and to spend their money.

The '60s marked the beginning of the end of the railroad bar car. New York commuter trains had bar cars since the early 1900s. A typical commuter train bar car was arranged with the bar at one end of the car, and upholstered chairs running the length of the car on each side. Some cars would include tables with seating for two on either side for playing card games, which ranged from bridge and pinochle to hearts and poker. The staff of the car consisted of only the bartender. In the first half of the 20th century, the customer could remain in his seat and merely push a button for service. By the '60s the buttons no longer worked, and you had to go to the bar to be served.

Riding in the bar car had a lot of advantages. Just like

any bar, it had a cadre of regular customers who were there five nights a week. Chairs were comfortable, especially when compared to the ones in a regular commuter car where you sat on a bench type seat, two abreast (side by side), often sharing with a stranger. Time passed more quickly in the bar car with plenty of conversation about the day's events, sports, family, jokes, and vacation plans.

In addition to the regular bar cars where there was usually only one bar car per train, there were private cars which had a seating arrangement similar to the bar car individual upholstered chairs, a few tables for card games, and a bar without a bartender. The members of the private car, who paid annual dues, in addition to their normal railroad ticket, served themselves from liquor stored in their individual lockers. Once again the advantage was being able to travel the hour or more each way with friends in comfortable surroundings.

Without question, there were people riding in the bar car because they "needed" a drink; however, they were a small minority. Friday nights, end of the workweek, especially in the summer, when people fled New York City for homes and rentals at the shore, were really memorable occasions. The bar car would be packed, crowded by any standard; and people would stand, and drink, and smoke, and talk for the entire trip, or until the train dropped passengers off at the various stops, and seats became available. The crowd from the bar car overflowed to the regular car behind the bar car, which on many occasions would be so full that the conductor could not navigate the aisles to collect the tickets.

Of course, there was no way the lone bartender located at the far end of the bar car could begin to serve a fraction of these people. The answer? They brought their own beer, wine and liquor, including mixes and ice. While the railroad bar car has disappeared, it has been replaced by bars on boats that take commuters to and from jobs in major cities.

It is difficult to determine where and when the idea for "Happy Hour" originated, but during the '60s it definitely became widespread in this country. And, in many places, the custom goes forward to this day.

There are any number of variations on the "Happy Hour" theme. The most common, of course, offers two drinks for the price of one, or all drinks half- price during a specific time period. For example, "Happy Hour" might extend from 11:30 A.M. to 2:00 P.M. to attract the luncheon crowd; or, it may begin at 4:00 P.M. and last till 6:00 P.M. to ensure a customer base before the evening crowd arrives.

In many places in the U.S., the "Happy Hour" custom came under intense scrutiny as a major source of drunken driving incidents. No doubt, for some people, two drinks for the price of one can easily lead to having four drinks, particularly if a few people on the way home from work decide to treat each other—worse if it is a group of people on the way home from work. This has led some locales and in certain instances, entire states, to ban the "Happy Hour" practice. To avoid this problem and save some money, the "Happy Hour" at many establishments offers free food in place of free drinks. It certainly reminds us of the food offerings discussed earlier under the Saloons chapter.

I fondly recall "Happy Hour" at the Officer's Club at Fort McClellan, Alabama in the '50s. First of all, the Officer's Clubs at these permanent military bases were quite impressive. This one had a large oval bar, in addition to a ballroom and various game rooms, swimming pool, etc. Drinks were 50 cents each, except during happy hour on Fridays from 4-6:00 P.M. when they were half-price. We shrewdly calculated that we were saving 25 cents per drink. Therefore, the more we drank the more we saved. If we drank enough, we would be able to purchase a new car with our savings.

Ft. McClellan served two important functions; it was the Army Chemical Corps School and Training facility—which was why I was there; and it was also the Women's Army Corps (WACS) basic training center.

One Friday afternoon, with "Happy Hour" in full swing, several of us rookie second lieutenants, were seated on one side of the bar, while a few WAC officers were occupying the other side. One, a captain, smoking a small cigar, shouted across the bar and challenged us to a martini drinking contest at 25 cents a drink. The contest ended when one of my companions collapsed and fell off the bar stool; so much for "Happy Hour" contests.

It's interesting that now, especially in Florida and other retirement areas, Happy Hours are known as "early birds" (in fact, the "early bird" has become the state bird of Florida), and applies mainly to discounts on food between 4 and 6:00 P.M.

Another casualty of the '60s, due to the accompanying anti-establishment movement of the younger generation, was the decline in private clubs. Country clubs, which had previously touted yearlong waiting lists, began to "search" for members, offering incentives to join just to keep their dining rooms afloat. Large cities, like New York, had numerous private clubs, many of them associated with eastern Ivy League colleges; i.e., Yale Club, Harvard, Princeton, The University Club, New York Yacht Club—all of these survived and are doing well today. Lesser-known ones merged or closed during the '70s.

Every town of any consequence had its City Club where the local professionals had their lunch and drinks, and pretty much ran the town. These places were also open for dinner and parties on special occasions.

Following World War II, there was enormous growth in all types of Clubs. The Veterans of Foreign Wars and American Legion clubs sprung up everywhere. The Moose, Elks, and Knights of Columbus all experienced growth. These places all had their own bars. All of these peaked in the '60s and '70s and have declined to their 1930s Depression year levels—about half their peak memberships.

One of the ways these clubs attempted to arrest the decline was to switch from all-male membership, and permit women to join. This certainly doubled their customer base, and initially gave a boost to membership numbers. Unfortunately, the women began to exit the clubs as rapidly as the men, and the decline in membership goes on.

Robert D. Putnam, Professor of Public Policy at Harvard University gave a speech at Chautauqua Institution, Chautauqua, New York on July 29, 2004, titled "Community Engagement in a Changing America." The message: in all forms of social interactions, formal and informal, the American people became less engaged during the last third of the 20th century.

Several national polling firms collect data monthly on personal behavior including church attendance, attendance at civic meetings, club meetings etc. They measure 12 kinds of activity; and every one of them has declined in a major way over the last 30 to 40 years. As one example, in 1957, 49% of people surveyed played bridge, now 5% do. All of these social interactions were on the rise until about 1965; then the fall began. What are the reasons for this decline in sociability, which, of course, affects barroom activity?

First, increased use of the automobile—time spent in the car commuting is time not available for having a drink on the way home from work. Dr. Putnam included television, of course. As he said, "most people watch the television show "Friends" instead of having them. Time spent in a sports bar watching a football game is not the same as time spent discussing the day's events with the fellow standing on either side of you at the bar.

Older Americans still socialize. They go to Church, they have friends over for dinner and cards, they go to their local bar, restaurant or club. But their children and grandchildren do not. Between 2000 and 2004 we lost about a million "sure" voters, and added three million "sure" non-voters; their grandchildren. This pattern appears to have changed in 2008.

While social engagement declined and, with it, attendance at the local Club and bar, the fascination with the American drinking establishment continued. Television's most popular shows were built entirely around bars, or included a bar as the main gathering place and feature of the show.

"Cheers" was a popular hit show in the 1982-1993 period, and the entire production took place in a Boston bar. Each show was a replica of real life in a neighborhood bar. The bartender interacted with the customer; customers related their problems or philosophies to the staff, or to each other. Pretty soon the characters established an identity, and you would look forward each week to hear about Norm's wife (who was always at home), or Cliff's (the postman) opinion or philosophy on some aspect of life, or the bartender's latest sexual exploits.

Another prime time, popular television show, and a favorite of mine, was "Northern Exposure" on CBS from 1990-1995. The show was about life in a small, rural, Alaskan village. However, it was filmed in Roslyn, Washington, a small town about one and a half hours east of Seattle. Hollings Bar was a feature of the show, and much of the action and dialog occurred in the bar. The actual tavern used for the scenes was the "Brick," which is still in operation in Roslyn, Washington today.

The interior of Hollings Bar on the show included a bathroom labeled "Guys and Dolls" with photos of, respectively, James Dean and Marilyn Monroe, walls cluttered with flags, animals' heads (moose head wearing a hard hat), photos of an Iditarod sled dog race, signs promoting Alaskan Vodka and Snow Cap Ale, and numerous other humorous items.

Today, the Brick is a frequent tourist attraction offering good pub food as well as a variety of local beers. The Brick is the oldest operating pub or tavern in the state of Washington. The grand back bar is over 100 years old. The place offers live music on weekends and is packed.

The most popular television show of the 1970s was "All in The Family" starring Carroll O'Connor as "Archie Bunker." On the show Archie retired from his "working class" job and opened a neighborhood bar. Archie was a typical Queens, N.Y., Irishmen with lots of firm opinions and prejudices.

Drinking patterns in the U.S. are constantly changing. In the '50s and '60s, and well into the '70s, the popular drink of choice was Scotch whiskey. The big names were Cutty Sark, J&B, and Dewars. As we entered the '70s, wine was beginning to take the lead. Beer has been the number one alcoholic beverage in America since the Civil War; 23.6 gallons per person in 1988, and rising to 30 gallons per adult over age 21 in 2006. That works out to a little under one 12-ounce can per day. It's interesting to note that two-thirds of all beer drunk in the U.S. is consumed between 4 and 8:00 P.M.—hence, the Miller Breweries advertising slogan "It's Miller Time." Another factoid: more beer is drunk on the 4th of July than on any other day of the year.

In the last quarter of the 20th century, drinking establishments spread to every imaginable location: airport bars, bars in theatres, bars on airplanes, and bars (can you imagine) in laundromats, casinos (open 24 hours a day), strip joints, hotels, boats, ships, and nowadays, even a private bar with your own key in your hotel room. Any place you could capture a customer with a little idle time on their hands, someone planted a bar.

Various areas of the U.S. continued to have their special styles of bars. In the rural West and Midwest, the roadhouse, honky-tonk and dance hall (called "pressure-cookers" in Texas, because housewives could cook something in the pressure cooker, a new device at the time, and sneak out for an afternoon at a dance hall, and still have dinner on the table when the "other-half" came home.) Working-class men and ethnic minorities continued to patronize their favorite local neighborhood bar. Skid-row bars have always provided a haven for the "down and out"—open from early morning to late at night—they only closed for a few hours to sweep or hose the joint out; nightclubs, cocktail lounges and hotel bars were the favorites in the larger cities. Into the '70s, people would congregate at their favorite watering hole in New York City, Chicago, San Francisco before commencing the long commute home.

1980s

"Electricity is made up of extremely small particles that you cannot see with the naked eye unless you have been drinking." — Dave Berry

Three separate events had an effect on the bar business during the 1980s.

First, the Vietnam War had ended and the United States began to find optimism after a rough decade in the '70s. With more discretionary income, a lot of the anti-establishment attitudes of the '60s and '70s began to disappear. Clubs began to become popular once again—especially golf clubs, always an expensive form of recreation. However, there were changes; many younger members changed the club bar scene. Unlike the old-time club members, they divided their time among many diversions—they were not at the club every day of the week.

The second change effecting the bar scene in America was the result of raising the minimum drinking age from 18 to 21 on a national basis. Previously this had been an area left entirely to the individual states. Growing up in New York State in the '40s and '50s the drinking age was 18. In nearby Pennsylvania, only nine miles away, the drinking age had always been 21. The result: a stream, of traffic, especially on weekends carrying teenagers from Bradford, Pennsylvania to Olean, New York.

Years later, when my own children were teenagers in New Jersey, the same situation was still taking place. New Jersey had a drinking age of 21. New York State continued to have the minimum age set at 18. The result, as much as we parents tried to discourage it, was cars carrying New Jersey youngsters to Staten Island, New York to drink and purchase alcohol.

As stated previously, part of the reasoning behind some states setting the minimum age at 18 was based on the minimum draft age being 18. "If you're old enough to go to war and be wounded or killed for your country, you're old enough to buy a drink." In 1984, this country was not at war!! By 1988, every state had raised its minimum drinking age to 21 spurred by their eligibility to receive federal highway funds.

Now, we are in the first decade of the 21st century, and the drinking age debate is on the table again. Partly this is the old question of 18-year-old soldiers killing and being killed in Iraq and Afghanistan; but, mainly it is a question of whether delaying drinking to age 21 is a good idea at all—in simple terms, it may create more problems than it solves. It is certainly no secret that the United States has an underage drinking problem of significant proportions. Producing fake ID is so rampant that it has become a cottage industry in the U.S.

The proponents of lowering the age limit base their position on the past, holding that the current law, like Prohibition, is unenforceable, and is universally ignored. It has forced drinking "underground." As noted earlier, a common practice, since these people can't drink legally in bars and clubs, is to get loaded as much as possible before going out—called "front-loading" or "pre-gaming."

A group has formed a movement titled "Choose Responsibility," which advocates teaching young people "how to drink," and "how not to drink." They favor a program that would tie qualifying for a driver's license to having a clean record regarding alcohol violations at age 18.

This approach is not a radical idea; only three other countries in the world restrict purchasing drinks to those age 21 and older—Mongolia, Palau and Indonesia. There are, of course, some countries that eliminate alcohol completely based on religious beliefs.

Mothers Against Drunk Drivers, MADD, which was the main force behind the 1984 law, is totally opposed to lowering the age limit. They point to a ream of studies showing a strong correlation between the higher drinking age and a reduction in teen-age drunk driving accidents.

In response, the Choose Responsibility group cites other

factors that may have contributed to the reduction in injuries and fatalities in alcohol related accidents—seatbelts, air bags, police check points, and the job MADD has done in stigmatizing drunk driving and alerting people to the consequences. They say the best way to reduce drunk driving among those under 21, is to raise the driving age, which is as low as 15 and 16 in many states.

The third item affecting the alcohol business in the '80s was the very formation of MADD (Mothers Against Drunk Driving). Founded in 1980 by Candy Lightner, and a small group of mothers in California, following the death of her teenage daughter by a repeat offender drunk driver. It's not a crusade against alcohol consumption. Its mission is to stop drunk driving, support victims, and prevent underage drinking. This has been a highly successful organization, and it has led to people realizing they are going to have to accept a lot more responsibility for their behavior while drinking. There was a time when the statement, "Oh, he was drunk," was accepted as an excuse for causing accidents while operating a vehicle. Not anymore!! Driving while under the influence of alcohol is a serious offense, even if you are not involved in a traffic accident. Law enforcement people routinely set up late night roadblocks to stop drivers and test them for alcohol levels in the blood stream. The minimum level in most states is now down to .08%; this translates to having two drinks in an hour or less. First time offences usually result in loss of driver's license for six months, and an insurance surcharge of several thousand dollars over a three-year period. A second or third offense can result in loss of license for a year or more and 30 or more days in jail.

The seriousness of DWI (driving while intoxicated) and DUI (driving under the influence) offenses, especially when a traffic accident is involved, has put an important burden on the bartender and bar owner. Lawsuits for the injured typically attempt to expand the responsibility beyond the driver to include those who served the drinks and to the bar where the drinks were consumed; they can even include companions in the vehicle who, perhaps, should not have let the individual drive the car. This has led to a popular custom of designating a driver who does not drink to handle the driving chores when the group goes out to party.

The latest wrinkle in the police approach to drunk driving is to determine where the driver consumed the last drink, called the "Last Drink Initiative." States like New Jersey, Washington and others have created an electronic data base by entering the names of the establishments cited by those stopped for DWI as the place they had their last drink of the day, or evening, or morning. Those places cited most often receive a visit, or several, from the State's Alcoholic Beverage Control Board.

Bar owners are upset about this new technique, claiming that drivers don't always provide truthful information. For example, if a husband or boyfriend has been drinking at "Lynne's Go-Go Bar," he's likely to tell the police he was somewhere else.

The ABC Board says they do not use the data to justify fines or license revocations, only to inspect the establishment for violations—and to call attention to troublesome spots that appear on the list too frequently.

Other states, Texas and Colorado, have used the data to warn certain bars to be more careful in regard to serving intoxicated patrons. At the end of each year, the Washington State patrol publishes a list of the most frequently mentioned "last drink" locations.

New Jersey police arrest about 32,000 drivers a year on suspicion of drunken driving, and more than 30% of accidents in the state involve allegedly intoxicated drivers.

The American Beverage Institute, representing restaurant and bar chains throughout the United States, worries that MADD's long-term objective is to eliminate drinking and driving completely; one drink would be considered DUI. For many years, it has been illegal in Sweden to drive after consuming any amount of alcohol—alcohol test must be zero.

Recently, in Florida, the adult children of an elderly couple brought suit against their parents' friends for serving their parents too much alcohol and allowing them to leave the party and attempt to drive home. The couple became disoriented and drove into a pond, resulting in their deaths.

MICRO BREWERIES AND CRAFT BEER

"Without question the greatest invention in the history of mankind was beer. Oh, I grant you the wheel was also a fine invention, but the wheel does not go nearly as well with pizza."
  − *Dave Barry*

Just as the beer industry in the U.S. was shrinking from the 3500 pre-Prohibition breweries to the 200 after Prohibition, to just a handful of major players since 1970, a new participant appeared on the scene. In 1977, the first microbrewery (so called because of the small size) opened. The New Albion Brewing Company, Sonoma, California, offered the first microbrew in 1977. The Sierra Nevada Brewing Company opened in 1981 in Chico, California; the microbrewery began its spread throughout the West, and eventually micros opened everywhere.

Prior to this event the only serious beer competition came from America's fascination with imported beer from Holland and Germany, then from Australia, Japan, and other foreign sources. But the microbrewery was not just a small beer brand; as it spread across the country, it included bars. The beer was actually brewed in the bar − "brewpubs." These have opened across the U.S., and are especially popular at resorts, particularly ski resorts. The brewpub is a sort of "home base" for the particular brand; but the beer is sold at retail locations and in bars in the local area.

Some of these micro-brews, of course, have grown into major brands, and, hence, are no longer exactly "micro-brews." One of these early brands was Samuel Adams, produced by the Boston Beer Company, and now the largest craft beer brewer in the U.S. followed by Sierra Nevada Brewing Company and the New Belgium Brewing Company of Fort Collins, Colorado.

In 1979, President Jimmy Carter signed a bill repealing restrictions on home-brewing small amounts of beer. Prior to this bill, there were 42 breweries in the U.S., today there are 1442, and 1390 are craft breweries. In addition, it is estimated that over 500,000 people brew their own beer using kits available in stores and catalogues throughout the country. On the popular "Drew Carey" television comedy show in the '90s, the star of the show brewed and sold beer in his garage—called "Buzz Beer."

These craft brewers experiment with all sorts of ingredients to alter the flavor—berries, special hops, and spices. This produces some very intense and distinctive flavors. The result is that beer is now becoming a lot like wine, where chefs are pairing these beers with certain meals and foods, and restaurants are conducting beer tastings. Wine is no longer the only beverage to be served with good food.

New Belgium beer went commercial in 1991, selling 220 barrels of beer and using hand labeling and bottling. Sixteen years later the beer is no longer made in the family's basement, and sales are projected at 485,000 barrels, or more than 124,000 cases per week. The brewery tasting room attracts 500 visitors a day. Instead of going to Napa Valley or the Finger Lakes Wine Trail, beer aficionados are visiting the nation's many craft breweries, brewpubs, and beer festivals.

Nearly every major city has a brewery these days, and Cleveland, Ohio is a good example. At the Great Lakes Brewery Company, locals have been gathering at the wonderful mahogany bar for over a century. But now on weekends the parking lot is filled with out-of-state plates. They come for a taste of the brewery's award winning Dortmunder Gold, a crisp lager. Great Lakes Brewery planned to produce 50,000 barrels in 2007, and is ranked by the Brewers Association, Boulder, Colorado, as the 26th largest craft brewery in the United States.

Another stop in Cleveland is the Brew Kettle Taproom, a short drive from Great Lakes Brewing. The Brew Kettle was voted by ratebeer.com as the number one brewpub in the country. Visitors can brew their own beer in the fermentation room, or select from an impressive variety of craft beers on tap.

Beer appreciation is a transformation in progress, another hobby.

It is now being judged, criticized and enjoyed with food by discriminating connoisseurs. It's not just a beer and a hot dog anymore.

Portland, Oregon now claims to have more brewers than any other city in the world, 31 breweries according to the Brewers Association. One local pub has over 100 beers on tap. The state of Oregon has only about 1% of the United States' population, but has over 7% of America's 1400 breweries and brewpubs. Nationally, craft brews make up about 3-4% of all beer sales, but in Oregon they make up almost 11% of statewide beer sales. Oregon craft beers tend to be on the dark side, and the trend is now moving toward the heavier-tasting ales —replacing the clear, bright lagers. Another unusual feature of Oregon beer sales is the strong draft beer market. Sixteen percent of the beer sold in the state is "on tap," as compared to about 3% in California.

The dominance of draft beer means small brewers can get started without expensive bottling equipment, so the many brewpubs can sell most of their output right on the premises. In total beer sales the state of Oregon is ranked 28[th,] with consumption of 31 gallons per capita, versus the national average of 31.3 gallons in 2006.

All these special beers are compared and rated at various websites (ratebeer.com) and festivals around the country. Ratebeer's website conducts semiannual surveys which include 30,000 beers from 4,000 breweries. Usually included in the top ten is a beer from St. Sixtus of Westvleteren, a Trappist monastery in Belgium. The abbey in Westvletern has been brewing beer since 1836, and only brews 60,000 cases per year. The beer has an alcohol content of 12%, versus a can of Coors, which is 4%. For a listing of beer festivals in the U.S. try "beeradvocate.com" and "ratebeer.com" websites.

Before extending the review of this all-important beer segment of the bar business, a description of the two main types of the major brands is worthwhile. The two basic styles of beer are ales and lagers.

Lagers are stored and take longer to ferment; the taste is clean and crisp. Pilsners are a type of lager, and tend to be pale golden with a bitter finish. Another subgroup, pale lagers are fuller and have a mild bitter finish. These include big-name U.S. brands—Budweiser, Miller Lite, and Coors. Ales are fuller-bodied and spicier. A subgroup includes the full-bodied, darker stouts, like the popular brand, Guinness.

The major beer producers in this country have welcomed the craft beers because of the excitement and interest they have brought to the whole market. The craft brewing industry has been growing over 10% a year for the past few years, and the microbreweries have had even stronger growth. A micro brewery is categorized as producing less than 15,000 barrels per year. In 2006, craft beer sales were up 17%, while all domestic beer sales rose 2%.

The three major brands: Anheuser-Busch, Miller and Molson-Coors continue to account for the bulk of beer sales, and beer continues to be the number one alcoholic beverage. But beer has lost market share to wine and spirits over the past10 years. Wine and spirits have been very successful in targeting the all important younger drinkers.

The beer industry has been fighting back, and sales have improved over the past two years, despite higher prices and shortages of grain. The increase is directly related to an increase in the population of eligible drinkers, and the growing popularity of the micro brews and craft beers. Current data show Americans consume over 30 gallons annually per capita for adults over twenty-one. States like Texas, Nevada, Montana, Wyoming, Louisiana and Mississippi consume almost twice as much beer as folks in California, New York, Connecticut and New Jersey.

The beer industry is dominated by Anheuser-Busch*, which has almost 50 percent of the market. Anheuser-Busch continues to concentrate its advertising and promotional efforts on the beer markets most sought after demographic—men ages 21 to 34. This means spending promotional dollars on sports, and Anheuser-Busch spends about 500 million a year on sports advertising. This includes being the exclusive alcohol advertiser on the Super Bowl, at $3 million for a 30 second commercial. Other events with a major Anheuser-Busch presence include the Kentucky Derby and Preakness horse races, Daytona 500 and NASCAR auto races, major league baseball, PGA golf, NCAA basketball tournaments and major college football. Anheuser-Busch strongly believes that the highest priority in marketing beer is the live sporting event.

Anheuser-Busch also has sizeable stakes in the craft beer category and the imported brands area, including Grupo Modelo, maker of the best selling Mexican import, Corona beer.

The top selling U.S. beer, by the way, is Budweiser, and the top selling lite beer is Bud Lite, and the total U.S. beer market exceeds $90 billion annually.

---

*Anheuser-Busch traces its roots back to the Bavarian Brewers founded in 1852 in St. Louis.
Anheuser-Busch is now owned by InBev, a Belgian company.

Now, after seeing the sales spurt of flavored distilled spirits, and craft beers with splashes of vanilla, citrus and berries, the mainstream breweries are introducing new beers, such as Bud Light Lime, Miller Chill, and Coors Blue Moon brand. Blue Moon offers seasonal flavors that include pumpkin for autumn, lime for spring, honey for summer and dark Belgian sugar for winter. Sales for the brand grew 51% in 2006, and it sells for $2 more per six-pack than the average $4.90 for Coors or Coors Light.

It's not surprising that the beer producers would want to get in on the action after seeing sales of flavored vodka grow 60% in the past five years. Absolute Vodka now comes in10 flavors including Pepper, Mandarin (orange), Mango, Vanilla, and even Pears.

I want to pay deserved tribute to two important additions to the American bar scene: craft beers and the captivating microbrewery. They are both on the upswing, and helping revive the popularity of the bar in the U.S.

In addition to small wineries, craft breweries and micro-brews, small-scale distilleries are now returning to the U.S. scene – and this time they are legal. These places are producing handcrafted vodkas, gins, bourbons, rye whiskies, and single malt whiskies.

Craft spirits remain a tiny niche in the U.S. spirits industry, averaging about 6,000 cases a year. The U.S. spirits industry totally rings up about $58 billion per year.

The Tuthilltown distillery, located in the Hudson Valley about 70 miles north of New York City, produces about 6,000 bottles of vodka and whiskey a year; but is hoping to double the amount when a new 250 gallon still arrives. These handcrafted products are not cheap, selling for $35 to $45 a bottle. But Tuthilltown remains sold-out, and the other 90 active craft distillers nationwide all seem to be doing quite well catering to America's desire for high-end spirits of all types.

The bar business, particularly in the downtown areas, remains extremely competitive. The owners compete by attempting to carve out their special niche. They may offer good food –"the thing about food and drink, you can drink anywhere, but you can't get slow smoked baby back ribs anywhere." People don't go around saying they had a great drink at "The Steer" last night; but they might say I had a great steak at "The Steer" last night.

Other bars may depend on entertainment to attract a particular clientele—rock music, DJ's, blues or jazz. Others adopt a theme; an Irish Pub, sports bar with 20 TVs, a piano bar with romantic soft music, etc.

Here's a sampling of the weekly autumn schedule at Bar Anticipation, located in lively Belmar, New Jersey—near the Atlantic Ocean.

Monday—Dinner night—$2 drinks and appetizers, dinner specials with celebrity chefs.

Tuesday—Beat the Clock—Miller Lite Draft Beer starts at 50 cents at 9:00 P.M., and increases 25 cents every half hour till 12:00 A.M. Dancing with DJ Dave. Jagermeister and shot specials 11:00 P.M.- 1:00 A.M.

Wednesday - Band Audition Night. See the areas hottest up-and-coming bands.

Thursday - Ladies Night. Drinks for ladies 75 cents till midnight; Karaoke Steve at 5:00 P.M. till 8:00 P.M.

Friday - Giant Happy Hour. Complimentary Buffet, Budweiser beer $2.25 all night.

Saturday - Great Bands. Dog Varies, Bitter X, The Zone, Life Speed. DJ Mike Nice between sets.

Sunday – Football, 40 TV screens and one giant screen. First drink free for ladies wearing football jerseys, plus free hot and cold buffet.

And on and on it goes. The following week included a return of "The Dueling Pianos" and a comedy show. Other competing bars in the area offered Sunday brunch for $10, happy hour prices, 21 different martini drinks, Italian Festival night every Thursday, All You Can Eat Roast Beef night—special coffee drinks, half price pizza nights, pool tournaments, dart contests, Latino Night, live FM Station broadcasts, every Tuesday Ladies Hot Body Contests with prizes. Bars are now sponsoring "take-offs" on the popular TV show, and have introduced "American Idol" contests.

The neighborhood tavern, that mainstay of the bar scene from the beginning, today has a tough time hanging in there. The dark, cool watering holes, where the laborers have dropped by for a drink on their way home from work, are disappearing as each year goes by, and so are the laborers! Chicago boasted of having over 7500 taverns in the early 1900s, and has just over 1300 today.

The neighborhoods have changed. At one time the north side of Chicago was filled with small neighborhood manufacturing plants that dotted the closely packed blocks of housing along with Catholic churches, schools and fire departments. Men walked to work and the neighborhood bar was the country club of the community.

The decline is similar in all the big cities—Boston, Philadelphia, and Cleveland. Elected officials are aiding the decline; no one wants to be seen as an advocate of a bar. The changing neighborhoods, with a growing number of upscale residents who would rather see a bistro than a bar on the corner, add to the demise of the old-fashioned bar.

In the beginning years of television, the bar was the only place to escape the sweltering summer heat, and watch a baseball game on the only TV set in the neighborhood. Now the bar is gone and some *chi chi* place is open, charging prices the old neighborhood could only imagine.

Recently a bar called "The Place" in Buffalo, New York announced that it was closing. The Place had been serving customers at the corner of Lexington and Ashland Streets since 1941. This is a beloved neighborhood bar and restaurant. It was founded by Bernie Flynn and the Moriarity family—father, uncle and son; and they have run it for the past 40 years.

There are Currier and Ives prints on the wallpapered

walls, and a special sandwich, Flynnie's Thinnie (Swiss cheese, ham and onion on thin rye bread), named for the founder. There are the traditions, like serving 2,000 pounds of corned beef on St. Patrick's Day, and thousands of Tom and Jerry's at Christmas.

This is the typical, wonderful neighborhood bar. Some people come five days a week; customers get engaged here. When a regular dies, his obituary will include he was a member of The Place. People have their special spots at the bar, or in a booth; generations have come here. The regulars include members of the Rich family, a wealthy Buffalo family with a fortune made in the substitute cream and dairy products business.

Well, the good news is the Rich family feels so strongly about the Place, they are going to buy it, and keep it running as the same neighborhood bar it has been for 64 years. The Rich's feel it is an important part of Buffalo life.

J.R. Moehringer describes a bar called "Dickens" in his 2005 book "The Tender Bar, A Memoir." This neighborhood bar was located in Manhasset, Long Island, New York. Quoting from his book: "Dickens was a bar that catered to multiple personalities. A cozy club one minute, a crazy after-hours club the next. A family restaurant in the early evening; late at night a low-down tavern. A place where everyone would feel special and no one would stand out. The burgers would be big, the closing time negotiable—no matter what the law said, and the bartenders would give an extra, extra, long pour, double the ordinary drink anywhere else.

"A Friday in the middle of August the bar contained a pageant of characters. There were priests and softball players, and executives from Manhattan. There were men in tuxedos, and women in gowns on their way to charity functions. There were golfers just off the links, sailors just off the water, and construction workers just off the job site. The bar was as crowded as a rush hour train, and long and narrow, just like a bar car."

This description of Dickens bar was from the '70s and '80s; but, thank God, similar places do exist today. Places where they know your name and what you drink. Places where you need to go almost every day or night, lest you might miss something!

These are places where you sit down and stack your money on the bar next to your drink; and the bartender takes what he needs on trust. Someone buys you a drink and you are "backed up on Joe or Jim or?" A shot glass upside down in front of you shows you have one coming.

The language for asking for another drink is special. It may be just touching the rim of the glass, nodding yes, saying, "do it again" or "once more."

There is still hope! An ad for a new bar opening "late spring/early summer 2008" in Rumson, New Jersey stated the following:

"Murry MacGregor's Publik House; an establishment which serves as the focal point of the community and a meeting place for locals to gather socially and conduct business, while enjoying a comfortable and friendly atmosphere, with abundance of good food, good drink and good music. Hoping to be all this and more!" Now, this is encouraging, sounds like an ad for a bar 200 years ago.

TIKI BARS

"Any woman can have the body of a twenty-one year old; if she's willing to buy him a couple of drinks." – Unknown

One of the theme restaurant bars of the '60s and '70s used a Polynesian look that carried through from the décor to the music to the waiters and waitresses, and most importantly, to the drinks. They featured concoctions based mainly on rum, and promoted them with super photos in a drink menu with names like "Singapore Sling," "Missionaries Downfall," and "Virgin's Delight." The menu described the contents of each drink, which came with a little flower, or a paper-folding umbrella. Typical bars had palm tree décor, indoor waterfalls, and Hawaiian music. Now, in the beginning of the 21st century, tiki bars are back.

Victor Bergeron launched the tiki bar craze by turning "Hinky Dinks," his rustic restaurant in Oakland, California, into a Polynesian themed hideaway, and renaming it after himself, "Trader Vic's."

Bergeron came up with the Polynesian theme after a visit to Tahiti; he's credited with inventing the Mai Tai rum cocktail in 1944. The ingredients consist of 1 oz. of light rum, 1 oz. of dark rum, 1 oz. triple sec, ½ oz. grenadine, ½ oz. of limejuice, ½ oz. orgeat syrup (almond flavored), a speck of pineapple, and a maraschino cherry.

Another strong force in the early days of the tiki bar, '30s and '40s, was Don Beach, founder of a chain known as Don the Beachcomber; all are gone, but Trader Vic's continues in operation.

Don Beach opened the first Don the Beachcomber's in Hollywood in 1934. The place was typical Polynesian, but Don Beach was an accomplished mixologist, and is credited with many original recipes for "Rum Rhapsodies." These were cosmopolitans and margaritas of their day. His most famous concoction was the original "Zombie," and the recipe was a closely guarded secret. This drink contained 11 ingredients including three types of rum and three different fruit juices.

All this is enjoying a "Polynesian pop" at the beginning of the 21st century—tiki bars are back. Some current outstanding tiki bars include:

- Mai Kai—Ft. Lauderdale, Florida—opened 1956 – Place is filled with tikis, many carved in the Pacific, floor show every night.
- Bahi Hut—Sarasota, Florida
- Bali Hai—San Diego—opened 1954

James Teitelbaum, author of "Tiki Bar Trip," suggests several tiki bars that have been around awhile.

- Hola Kahilai – River Grove, Illinois – Chicago suburb
- Tiki-Tio—Los Angeles, tiny, family room bar with great drinks
- Tonga Room – Fairmont Hotel – San Francisco. This is an especially good tiki bar built around what used to be a swimming pool. So there's a lagoon room in the middle of the restaurant, and there's a rainstorm every half hour with a soundtrack and light show of thunder and lightning.
- Forbidden Island – Alameda, California – This place is only a few years old, but very well done.
- Trader Vic's – Hilton Hotel, Atlanta, Georgia

ST. PATRICK'S DAY

"An Irishman is the only man in the world that would step over the bodies of a dozen naked women to get to a bottle of stout." –
Brendan Behan

One of the highlights of the bar scene in America is St. Patrick's Day. Certain cities in this country are favorites for this Irish holiday, including Savannah, Georgia, Chicago and, of course, New York City. Studies have shown that among the major white American ethnic groups, Irish are the most likely to be drinkers (only 8% were abstainers), and are more likely to consume three or more drinks of hard liquor at a sitting. Combine this with St. Patrick's Day, when everyone pretends to be Irish, and you have the ingredients for a rambunctious bar scene.

In New York City the parade is over three hours long and shown on television, so it is available in every bar in the Northeast.

Bars with names like Flanagan's, Dooley's, Harrigan's, and O'Neill's, are full by noon, and stay packed until closing, whenever that may be! The more ambitious places feature Irish entertainment and Irish pipers, dancers, singers, and comedians. Others depend upon green beer, corn beef and cabbage, and decorations provided by the beer and liquor companies.

A St. Patrick's Day spent in a typical Irish bar, like Briody's in Rumson, New Jersey, was to say the very least, a memorable experience. The place opened at 10:00 A.M.; this barely gave them time to clean the place from the night before. You see, the St. Patrick's Day celebration in an Irish bar now extends to at least a week. Parties are scheduled every night for the week leading up to St. Patrick's Day. Upon opening, the places at the bar fill immediately. With one of these seats you can watch the day unfold as the celebrants come in for drinks and lunch, and then prepare for the evening. In between, you can watch the New York City St. Patrick's parade on television. On a typical St. Patrick's Day, a limo may arrive at 11:00 A.M. with six to eight guys drinking and smoking cigars. Their plan is to spend the day visiting as many Irish bars on the Jersey Shore as possible – they'll probably buy a memento t-shirt or hat in each one. They don't intend to quit until the next day; now staying sober enough to visit Irish bars from morning till night requires some drinking skill . . . hence, the limo! Another group may arrive dressed in so much green and Irish costume that it looks somewhat like Halloween.

By mid-afternoon, with the parade winding down, and a little lull between lunch and dinnertime, it's time for a visit of fairly decent Irish singers. Of course, the entire bar joins in this tradition of all the American favorites: "Harrigan," "Peg-O-My-Heart," "When Irish Eyes are Smiling," and even a few Irish folk tunes. The finale is always "Danny Boy."

The highlight of the evening at any one of these bars— that is, in addition to the fact that you can't hear yourself think because people are four deep at the bar and no one can enter unless someone leaves—you now need boots to enter the restroom, where at least one of the toilets has overflowed, and at least one of the amateurs has been sick. Then the evening is highlighted by a visit of the Irish pipers. These guys get paid to go from bar to bar, enter the front door playing, circle the entire barroom a couple of times and exit in the rear. Their normal everyday function is to appear at Irish funerals and weddings.

So what do we all do for the rest of the evening? Well, there are stories to tell, stories and tales from past St. Patrick's Days, stories from someone who spent last St. Patrick's Day in Dublin, or Savannah, or Boston, or Chicago. Then there are the new arrivals at the bar, people who have spent the day in New York watching the parade, or (God be praised!) even working. They always have new input about a "happening" in the city, or on the commuter train or boat. Be assured there is no lack of conversation— these Irish can talk as well as drink.

And let's not forget the Irish jokes—my goodness, they

213

are a part of every day, but especially appropriate on St. Patrick's Day. Here are just a few: an Irishman stays at the pub until closing, and can't seem to stand or walk; so he crawls home and sneaks into bed. He is awakened next morning by his wife shouting, "Paddy, you were down to that pub last night, weren't you?" Paddy replies, "Are you sure of that?" She shouts, "The pub just called and said that you left your wheelchair down there again."

A little Irishman leaves the pub on St. Patrick's Day and finds someone has painted his horse green. He marches back into the pub and shouts, "Who the hell is the smart ass that painted my horse green?" Biggest, toughest guy in the bar stands up and says, "I did, what about it?" Little guy says, "I think he needs a second coat."

In Ireland, a priest enters a pub and announces: "Everyone who wants to go to heaven, stop drinking and stand up." Everyone stands up except Paddy. Priest says, "Paddy, don't you want to go to heaven someday?" Paddy says, "Someday. Oh sure, Father. I thought you were getting a group together to go now."

In the latter part of the 20th century all things Irish had taken their turn at popularity; and the Irish Pub, always beloved in areas of large Irish populations, such as Boston and New York City, has become popular throughout the United States. Irish-themed movies were popular in the '50s, now its Irish dancers (Riverdance), Irish tenors, Irish beer (Guinness) and Irish bars.

Guinness, the world's leading brewer of Irish beers, located in Dublin, inaugurated an Irish Pub Concept program to capitalize on the popularity of "all things Irish." Their goal, of course, is to sell more Guinness Stout in the United States.

Through its relationships with designated designers and builders, Guinness has assisted in the opening of several thousand so-called "authentic" Irish pubs around the world, and over 100 in the United States.

The Guinness affiliates, the Irish Pub Co., and the Irish Pub Design and Development Company, have built these pubs and shipped them to over 40 countries, including the Matsumote

Irish Pub in Japan, and Shanghai O'Malley's in China. Maybe we're ready for an Irish-themed Chinese restaurant in San Francisco.

The Irish Pub Design Co. lets customers select which "authentic" version of a faux pub they prefer; the cottage pub, the old brewery house, the shop pub, the Gaelic pub, the Victorian pub or the contemporary pub.

The bars and accompanying décor are built in Ireland, shipped to this country, and assembled by a crew sent over from Ireland. When the pub opens, Guinness provides an Irish bartender to help set the proper Irish tone for the "pub." Of course, not all the Irish-themed pubs opening in America are built in Ireland; most are constructed here to look like an Irish pub. The accompanying décor, menu, music and television are usually the same.

The menu will have a traditional Irish breakfast served all day—eggs, rashers (a traditional Irish sausage), black and white pudding, tomatoes and brown bread. Dinner options include salmon, fish and chips (sounds British), shepherd's pie and lamb stew. The television will offer sporting events directly from Ireland, Gaelic football, soccer and hurling.

The whole idea is to make you feel as though you are at home in a real Irish pub as soon as you step through the door. In order to accomplish this, the bar must have a regular customer base that loves to hang out there and enjoy the television, music, beer, and most of all, the conversations.

Another well-financed group of Americans has gone one step further. They are actually purchasing pubs in rural corners of Ireland and shipping the interiors to America for re-assembly in Irish hot-spots like Boston, Chicago, Savannah, Buffalo and New York City.

There is even an authentic Irish pub at Downtown Disney in Disney World, Raglan Road. Walt Disney, who prohibited alcohol on all his properties, must be rolling over in his grave!!

Two Irish bars in downtown Buffalo, New York show how competitive and changing the bar business can be.

In the year 2004, the Dublin based designers for Guinness, built and installed the interior components of "D'Arcy McGee's" Irish-themed bar/restaurant in downtown Buffalo. Now, D'Arcy McGee's is changing to a blues and barbecue-themed venue. Meanwhile, 10 blocks away, work is progressing on "W.J. Morrissey's Irish Pub," set to open next year. Once again the bar is designed by Dublin-based Gemmal, Griffon and Dunbar, and will include all the touches of a pub right out of the "old sod," including a "snug" that will open at 6 A.M. to serve breakfast and lunch. The exterior will make you think you are in the middle of County Cork. A "snug," by the way, was the small, enclosed room in the corner of an Irish pub where women were allowed to drink, since they were not permitted at the bar until the 1960s. The beer was passed through a small window in the snug by the bartender. Most of the time he had no idea who was drinking it.

TODAY'S BAR

"There are no strangers here, only friends you haven't met"
—William Butler Yates

The following is a description of an "up-to-date" urban bar in 2006. Upon entering the bar the first thing you may encounter are a couple of very large bouncers who will scrutinize your ID if you're under forty. From there you have lots of choices—a round of billiards, darts, foosball, air hockey or an array of arcade games.

If you turn right at the entrance you'll probably find a long bar served by scantily clad young ladies in uniform outfits. Beyond the bar is the dance floor with a disc jockey, plenty of mirrors, strobe lights and loud music. The weekends will include a live band, and every night of the week will feature something special, i.e., ladies night, two dollar drafts night, free pizza, etc.

So, you can see the typical today's "young crowd" bar has something for everyone: booze, games, music, dancing; even if you try hard, some conversation. Even in a mid-size town the hours are seven days a week, until 4 A.M., kitchen open till 2 A.M.

Bar owners have been creative, inventing special nights or events and even weeklong celebrations. On a recent trip to Key West, Florida, it happened to be the 5th of May, Cinco de Mayo, a Mexican holiday. The drinking establishments of Key West had turned this into a weeklong celebration. Just a sample review of three bars will give you an idea of the activities.

The Hog's Breath Saloon, whose motto is "Hog's breath is better than no breath at all," was conducting a bartending contest, which was going to last most of the week, with a $1,500 first prize. The idea was for local bartenders to appear individually on an improvised stage in the bar where all the ingredients for a special "tropical concoction" had been assembled. This was a test of speed and quality. The drink prepared by the contestant (all qualified bartenders) was then poured out to the judges assembled throughout the bar crowd, and wearing cups strung around their necks into which the drink was poured.

At the Schooner Wharf Pub an entirely different contest was taking place on the same evening. The Schooner is an open-air bar with a mostly dirt floor and umbrellas over the tables and a makeshift roof over the bar—real Key West. An FM radio disc jockey with a microphone had selected five young guys from the crowd, and they were seated at a table facing the audience. The point of the contest was to find which one of the five could down a shot of Tequila, one Corona beer, three large tacos, and a chili pepper in the shortest time period; this was followed by five females doing the same thing. In fact, of the ten contestants, a woman was the fastest. Now this was early in the evening and it was only "Round One." It was really a funny event with the crowd shouting for their favorites, and plenty of off-color comments from the guy with the microphone, including commenting on the size of the peppers the girls were swallowing, and the girls responding that "size does matter."

Meanwhile at Sloppy Joe's Saloon, just down the street from The Schooner, a band was performing with a vocalist singing a song I certainly had never heard. The object of this contest was for selected members of the crowd to come up on stage, and each time the vocalist came to an off-color, i.e., filthy word, in the lyrics, the contestant had to substitute sign or body language. Try this and you can readily see that with a few drinks it could become really funny. This is an example of just three bars in a town containing at least 50 and all of this took place early in the evening.

Other more commonplace, or regular, bar entertainment includes wet t-shirt contests for the ladies, karaoke singing featuring anyone in the bar and a D.J., and, of course, traditional bar music of guitars, pianos, trios, and keyboards.

Also "ladies nights" are popular—women are either admitted at no-charge if there is an entertainment cover charge, or drinks are half price for ladies. This, of course, attracts the women, which attracts the men.

Sports bars have zoomed since the arrival of satellite TV. Now, on a given Sunday in autumn a bar with enough TV sets can broadcast every game being played in the National Football League. Tully's Good Time Bar in Amherst N.Y. has 82 television sets. The bars offer special beer prices, tailgate party food, such as chicken wings with hot, hot sauce, pizza or Mexican food to go with Corona beer (the number one import), hot dogs, hamburgers, sushi bars and raw seafood bars. There are all you can eat buffets for $10. Some bars feature prizes: t-shirts, special beer glasses, surf boards, snowboards—(seasonal) and football jerseys.

Sports bars became popular in the '50s and '60s and were often owned or operated by some local, sports celebrity. It could be a wrestler, boxer or football player—the more manly the sport the better. Then it became popular for sports stars to lend their names to places they never set foot in. It's amazing but the idea draws people—in Florida there is a line of Dan Marino bars, Miami Dolphins quarterback of the '90s; Don Shula steakhouses abound in honor of the Miami Dolphins Coach in the '80s and '90s. In New York there is a Mickey Mantle bar. St. Louis has a Stan Musial restaurant. Most of these fatigue as the "name" fades with time.

Some bars feature a different band seven nights a week. This tends to attract folks who favor a particular musical group. The band schedule for all the popular bars appears in the newspaper the prior week, and fans follow the band from bar to bar.

Theme nights are single nights, family nights, game nights, DJ dance nights, poker nights, shuffleboard, darts, and billiards.

A bar in New Jersey called the Cue and Brew is one of the more unique spots. It's two floors of pool tables, video games, and air hockey tables—rivals an amusement park arcade.

"Dave and Busters Grand Sports Café," of Dallas, Texas

is a national chain of 50 or more "stores" that combine sports, food, and drink on a large scale. Each location has 30-40,000 square feet of blinking lights, music, and plasma screen televisions, tables for drinking and eating, and spots for game playing. There's enough room for 400-600 people to wander around and enjoy bowling lanes, billiard tables, Pac Man videos, or use the "gambling-style" machines piled high with gold coins. A few new twists include the following: a photo booth that morphs instant pictures of couples into a "photo guess" of what a future child might look like! A television quiz show area lets people compete and answer programmed questions. A row of race car games with drivers' seats and television screens can be linked so friends can drive cars into each other's screens. There are private party areas, and a restaurant that has an 80-foot plasma TV screen. It's billed as a place for adult recreation. A place like this typically employs 170 to 200 people, not your regular neighborhood bar. It even has a "ticker tape" sign that continuously posts scores and game times around the world.

"Billy Bob's" bar in Ft. Worth, Texas with over 120,000 square feet, equal to three acres, has long been touted as the biggest bar in the country. It can handle over 6,000 customers and has 32 bars, 2 of which are over 100 feet long. In addition to the normal dance floors, video games, and slot machines, this place has a full-scale indoor rodeo arena, and beer accounts for 68% of the sales.

It's interesting how the establishment keeps track of the liquor sales. Not wanting to use liquor guns or hoses as too impersonal, or measuring devices on top of the bottles, Billy Bob's weighs the bottle at the beginning and end of each bartender's shift. The number of drinks, the size of the drinks and the cash received have to equate. For beer sales, the bottles are merely counted at the beginning and end of each shift. Unlike some places that brag about having over 100 beers available, Billy Bob's carries only 17 varieties.

Club La Vela in Panama City Beach, Florida, a spring break landmark, bills itself as "the largest nightclub in the

U.S.A." This place has room for 6,000 patrons in at least ten theme rooms and 38 bar stations. Alas, La Vela may soon be torn down to make way for more condominiums.

Patio bars are a growing and welcome addition to the bar scene. Long popular in Europe, these outdoor drinking areas seem to sprout like dandelions when spring arrives in towns like Boston, Cleveland, Chicago and Buffalo. People in this climate, of course, flock to an opportunity just to be outdoors on a beautiful evening.

The patio typically extends out onto the sidewalk where local ordinances permit this type of building extension. This gives the customers the chance to drink and watch the crowd go by. The best ones are located on downtown avenues that have several located within an easy stroll. This affords the folks a chance to barhop and survey the passing scene all night. A new twist on patio bars includes drinking facilities located on the roof of some buildings in major cities.

One unique feature of New Orleans' bars is the "to go" drink. A stack of plastic cups near the bar exit can be used to empty your drink from the drinking glass into the cup, called a "go cup." Then you are able to stroll along Canal Street, or wherever, sipping your cocktail. Some bars have "walk-up" windows where you can purchase a drink "to go" in a plastic container. Most cities and states prohibit the sale or consumption of alcohol in this manner; although regulars at bars frequently purchase a "roadie" or "one-for-the-road." Unfortunately, these drinks are usually consumed in vehicles on the drive home.

The Barrel House in Buffalo, New York has over 100 motorcycles parked out front on a typical evening. Wednesday is "Hawgs and Honeys" night. This is a nice bar—bartenders are friendly and the drinks are cheap. The crowd is "age-appropriate"—translated: "a grown-up can go there and not feel she's old enough to be everyone's mother!!" The fryer stays on all night, and the people are in their '40s. There's a patio out back for the smokers, and the jukebox has a selection to satisfy everyone. Every now and then someone buys a bucket of chicken wings ($17.75), and treats the bar. Tomorrow night will be some other special attracting folks from the Thursday night "Downtown on the Square" entertainment. The hours are interesting—7 P.M. to 4 A.M.; and I used to tell my kids "remember, nothing good happens after midnight."

Earl's in Sebastian, Florida is another "biker bar." Here the dress code includes tattoos, piercings, tank tops and well-worn jeans or jean skirts. On a typical weekend, hundreds of motorcycles will be parked at Earl's. Drinking is not confined to the original bar; it extends to the outdoor tiki bars.

For the past 20 years, another annual event has taken over the bar scene in this country—Halloween. Halloween had been a wonderful, scary and mischief-filled holiday for children for most of the 20th century; now it has expanded to include adults with parties at home, at clubs, and especially at bars. Enterprising bar owners offer special drinks, elaborate Halloween decorations and prizes for best costumes. The drinking, combined with the outfits, and especially the disguises, make for a fun-filled evening.

The gay population of this country has turned Halloween into a virtual Mardi Gras celebration in places like New York's Greenwich Village, Chicago's Rush Street, and Key West's Duval Street, where the festivities last a full week and the costumes are "unbelievable."

The one group that has been able to claim a share of the drinking market is the national restaurant chains. Friday's, Bennigan's, Olive Garden, and Applebee's have been very successful in establishing a bar business in the suburbs. These places have the power of national advertising campaigns to gain recognition. Marketing is sophisticated and food and drinks follow the "what's popular now" plan. At the moment it's a Mexican theme – and "American" Mexican food (which is moderate in price for the quantity delivered), tacos, fajitas, and burritos.

For reasons already discussed, DWI and health consciousness, people are drinking less in bars and restaurants, but spending more. The martini is once more back in style. In the '50s and '60s the famous "three martini lunch" was big in major cities like New York, Chicago, and San Francisco. Following a lunch like that there wasn't much you could or should do but hang around till it was time to catch the bar car commuter train home.

Now, with people having one martini, they tend to go for the "top shelf" stuff. At the Peninsula Hotel Bar in Los Angeles the $18 martini has appeared on the menu. In fact, if that's not expensive enough, they also have a $26 margarita. Just a few years ago, $10 seemed to be the upper limit for a bar drink. Now you can find $15 martinis all over the bars in every major city. Even smaller towns may have at least a dozen different martinis and margaritas on the menu at $12 a pop. Some of these, of course, are not your run-of-the-mill martinis; they use top-of-the-line gin or vodka, like Grey Goose, Absolute or Belvedere – stuff that sells for $20 a bottle to the bar owner.

A typical special martini may have vodka, cranberry juice, and triple sec in a frosty glass full of dry ice; so, you get a bit of a show when a cloud of mist bellows from the glass. Other martinis may have raspberries floating on the top or olives stuffed with blue cheese, or any number of flavored vodkas; from apple to citrus, delivered to your table in a shaker and poured with a flourish.

Wine marketers are able to exploit today's snob appeal and have made the $10 glass of wine "ordinary." Five years ago a glass of wine competed with beer as the cheapest drink on the menu–not any more.

The appeal of martinis – or at least vodka-based drinks served in martini glasses, has proved to be even more profitable than wine for the bars and restaurants. Unlike wine, which requires careful storage and expertise and spoils in opened bottles, hard liquor is easy to buy, store and serve; especially vodka. It costs a distiller about 93 cents to create a gallon of vodka. Some of it sells for more than Johnny Walker Scotch that is aged in wooden barrels for 12 years. Vodka, you make it, fill the bottle, and ship it out the door; no aging involved. And vodka being just about tasteless, especially the more expensive, heavily filtered brands, mixes with just about anything.

So, as an example, a bar buys a quart of Absolute vodka for $20, or lesser brands for around $12. You can get about 20 drinks at 1½ ounces each out of a bottle. If you are charging $10 a drink, that's $200 from a $20 bottle. No wonder the bar is the profit center in these posh restaurants.

As Americans prefer these high-priced drinks, there is no end to the fancy cocktails being introduced on a daily basis. Fancy bars in the large cities are attempting to establish their "signature" drink, i.e., "The Elderflower Melon Cup" ($11.50) at the Park Hyatt in Washington, D.C., made with pureed melon, elderflower syrup, vodka and champagne, or Champagne Napoleon.

For a new "high-water" mark in pricing, a regular martini made with bargain booze, recently costs $21.50 including tax, at the King Cole Room bar at the St. Regis hotel in New York City. That's a "regular" martini – nothing fancy!!

SMOKING

"A guy turns to the fellow next to him at the bar and says, "Does your penis burn after you've had a couple of martinis?" Fellow replies, "I don't know, I have never tried to light it."—Unknown

The past 20 years have drastically changed smoking habits in America. The United States Surgeon General officially linked smoking to lung cancer in 1964; the evidence has increased significantly since. In addition, smoking is linked to other health problems including heart disease. More recently, scientific evidence has established a relationship between lung cancer and "second-hand" smoke.

Once this knowledge became widespread, it was only a matter of time before the public began demanding separation of smokers and non-smokers. At first this led to designating smoking areas in the workplace, then other public places including restaurants. Now, entering the 21st century, people are demanding legislation eliminating smoking in public, period!

It is hard for any older person to imagine a bar without smoking. That is what bars were all about. Pipes, cigars, cigarettes, chewing tobacco—these have been a major part of the bar scene from the beginning. Well, not anymore!

Despite furious protests from bar owners and restaurants, cities first and now entire states have outlawed smoking in enclosed public places: including bars and restaurants. Smoking is not allowed for example in any bar or restaurant anywhere in the state of New York. As usual, with laws governing the sale of alcohol, other states, cities, towns and counties throughout the United States have established their own rules. But it appears that eventually, as strange as it may seem, smoking in a bar is going to disappear, just as chewing tobacco and the spittoon disappeared 100 years ago.

The outcome of all this has defied the dire prediction of the alcohol industry of thousands and thousands of bankruptcies

225

and revenue losses. The no-smoking ban has actually increased business in most areas of the industry and, overall, the outcome has been a positive one.

In Europe, where smoking has not dropped off as much as in this country, and where smoking in a bar is about as commonplace as drinking in a bar, the change has been slow and surprising. In Holland, the drinking establishments are affectionately known as "brown bars." This is because the typical interior is "tobacco brown" from the centuries of smoking.

In Ireland, where the pub has been the hub of life for generations, smoking in pubs was banned throughout the country in 2004—no exceptions. People did not believe it would work, especially in the rural areas, but it has been successful and the pubs are surviving nicely. Of the estimated 10,000 pubs in the Republic of Ireland, 88% are family owned, the surnames spelled out in block letters above the front door—McCarthy's, O'Toole's, and Donovan's. First licensed in 1635, Irish pubs now answer to more than 80 separate laws that regulate the drinking trade.

Ireland, of all the countries on earth, long closely associated with drinking, especially in pubs, is now taking additional steps to clamp down on alcohol consumption. Ireland is currently a leader in DWI enforcement, which is why in small rural villages at the end of the evening you will find a crowd at a taxi stand waiting for a ride home. New laws aimed at public drunkenness ban happy hours, impose stiff fines on bartenders serving inebriates, and crack down on underage drinking.

If all that weren't enough, the government now requires health warnings on alcoholic drinks and limits on liquor advertising. Alcohol ads are banned on public transportation, and at cinemas and sporting events; no alcohol advertising on television before 10 P.M. All this in a country where 10,000 pubs serve a population of 3.8 million; and where Guinness Brewing Company sponsors the national soccer squad, and Heineken has the rugby team.

However, all is not lost: a nursing home in Ireland has installed a pub on the premises. Ready access to a nip, the theory goes, will lift the spirits of residents and may help them (average age 85) live longer. And, I find this to be interesting – "the pub has resulted in a significant increase in loved ones visiting the residents."

WHAT'S AHEAD?

"I never met a man I liked who didn't drink"—Will Rogers

The bar in this country has been in existence for over 300 years—from the very beginning. It changes every now and then; but the basic purpose for its existence remains the same. It serves the fundamental needs of millions of human beings—not all, but certainly at one time or another, a significant number.

In colonial times it was the very center of the town, serving the inhabitants' every need, from food and drink to Church and lodging. As the country grew, the tavern assumed roles as post office, courthouse, and eventually the birthplace of the Revolution. Stagecoach taverns appeared when they were needed to aid travelers as the United States expanded. Taverns were built along the canals when they became popular in the 1800s. When the railroad arrived, the tavern appeared right alongside the town railroad depot.

With the end of the Mexican War in 1846, and the discovery of gold in California two years later, the West opened with a rush. Boomtowns popped up from Denver and Leadville, to Deadwood, Tombstone and San Francisco. The first structure to appear in a boomtown was always the saloon. At first, it might be a tent or a wagon, but shortly thereafter, a building housing a bar appeared—made from whatever materials were available. Once again, the saloon served needs way beyond drinking; it was the bank, the post office, the courthouse, often the funeral parlor. When the boomtown went "bust," as they often did, the saloon was the last business in town to close its doors.

Even the "grand noble experiment" of Prohibition could not close the American bar. It changed, adapted, went under cover, and emerged 13 years later stronger than ever.

Following World War II, and the introduction of television and air conditioning, the bar was the only place for many ordinary people to see this newest marvel in comfort.

As we enter the 21st century, the American bar continues to slowly evolve. Just as back in colonial days, over 200 years ago, bars continue to be patronized by different classes of people.

Today, we still have the neighborhood bars, but they are disappearing slowly. The "club" remains for the exclusive use of its members—it may be a fraternal club (Elks, Moose, etc.), a golf country club, a downtown dining club, ethnic clubs (Irish, Polish, Italian), or yacht clubs. It is endless. There are now gay and lesbian bars for social contact among homosexuals. There are singles bars for heterosexuals seeking social contact with the opposite sex. We have the sports bars directed primarily at the all-male crowd. Nightclubs have reached a new height with the gambling casinos of Las Vegas, Reno and Atlantic City. These places are "posh," and feature top current entertainers.

Consumption of alcoholic beverages had been increasing for several decades prior to the 1980s—but the increase in the minimum drinking age from 18 to 21, a growing health consciousness in the U.S., and concern over the negative effects of alcohol among the better educated segments of the population—combined with state and federal governments increased tendency to raise funds through higher "sin taxes" on tobacco and alcohol—all these drove a decline in alcoholic beverage consumption. In addition, the emphasis placed on policing drunk driving had a profound effect on consuming alcohol outside the home.

Commenting on "sin taxes," it is worth noting that surveys have shown that about one-third of the U.S. population abstains from alcohol, another one-third drinks only occasionally, and the remaining third accounts for most of the alcohol consumed. With numbers like these, it is easy to see why politicians find it attractive to increase taxes on alcohol; it has practically no impact on two-thirds of the voting population.

Commenting on drinking statistics: of the percentage that drink alcohol, more are men than women, although the gap has been closing in recent years. Also reflected in these numbers is the beer and liquor advertising done by the industry and by individual bars. Drinking by men peaks at around age 30; women tend to drink most heavily after age 40; the beer ads are macho for the men; the fine wine ads appeal to more sophisticated women.

Why do people drink and why do they drink in a bar? We have seen that people drink for different reasons; and they have been doing it as long as historical records exist – we know the Greeks and the Romans had bars. And, of course bars are not unique to the United States, in fact they were copied from European drinking places that existed before this country was formed. Pubs, taverns, bistros, "brown bars," beer gardens—all thrive today in Ireland, Great Britain, Holland, France, Germany, Italy.

Coffee houses are the rage now at the beginning of the 21st century. People gather to talk, even read and socialize over a cup of "special caffeine." But, for obvious reasons, the coffee house is not a bar.

Worldwide, despite the diversity of drinking practices, there is a remarkable similarity in the way people use alcohol. There are six different functions of drinking customs—medicinal, religious, social, recreational, dietary and symbolic.

Symbolic—the choice of alcoholic beverage and the way it is consumed communicate a lot about the personality of the drinker. Advertisers are aware of the symbolic value of premium beers, fine wines and expensive whiskies. Young men want to project a certain "macho" image by drinking a certain beer; while women may wish to appear sophisticated by ordering an expensive wine. Certainly the amount of expensive wine, vodka and scotch sold in this country far exceeds the amount that could be consumed by customers who have developed educated tastes to appreciate these beverages. This has been confirmed every time a taste test is performed on a random group of drinkers. You would have a sure bet if you said 9 out of 10 wine drinkers could not select a $50 bottle of wine from a $10 bottle. In a recent test conducted by a well-known food magazine, blindfolded panel members were unable to distinguish between white and red wines—7 out of 10 were incorrect. A test by the New York Times food experts rated Smirnoff number one ($15) per liter, and Grey Goose far down the list and selling at $29 per liter.

"Great people talk about ideas, average people talk about things, and small people talk about wine." – Fran Lebowitz, 1950.

The medicinal benefits of alcohol have been discussed since medieval times. Today, it is scientifically recognized that a glass or two of red wine is good for the human heart. It has not been proven how good seven, or even eight, glasses are for easing mental stress.

The religious functions of drinking alcohol are evident in the rituals developed by some of the world's major religious groups. Wine is incorporated into the holiest ceremonies of the Christian and Jewish religions; and religious festival drinking occurs in many European countries.

Social drinking dictates which beverage may be chosen for the occasion—such as champagne for a wedding toast, beer for a tailgate party, wine with a fine dinner. Cocktail parties are occasions for copious drinking; but drunkenness is considered inappropriate. Fraternity parties, on the other hand, are occasions where intoxication and wild behavior are acceptable—even expected.

Recreational drinking occurs after work, on Friday nights, or at a sports event. Beer at a football game is practically part of the event; hot dogs and beer at a baseball game, a round of beer while bowling.

Dietary use of alcohol includes beverages accompanying a meal. The use of alcohol to accompany food has been developed to a fine art by the French. Food and wine must be matched harmoniously. To do this properly one must follow a prescribed ritual, which dictates the appropriate beverage to accompany each part of the meal. To open a meal and stimulate the appetite, one first takes an aperitif, such as vermouth, Pernod or Anise. During the meal, one chooses red, white or rose wine to complement the main course. Another wine may be called for when the cheese arrives, and champagne or sparkling burgundy may be ordered for dessert wine. Following the meal, a "digestif" or liqueur, or brandy, is usually taken to aid digestion.

So, these are the six different functions of drinking customs, the same all over the world, symbolic, religious, social, religious, recreational, and dietary. These help explain why and how people consume alcohol; but why do they go to a bar? We no longer go there to cash a check, be part of a jury, attend a funeral, or pick up our mail. But there are still a lot of reasons and excuses to go to your favorite bar. I have listed 16 thoughts below; and I am sure you can easily add your favorite to the list.

1. To relax and enjoy a drink before dinner.
2. To meet with friends and play pool, shuffleboard or darts—or watch a favorite team on television.
3. To unwind and have a drink after work, sometimes alone, and often with friends.
4. For single people, and I suppose for some who are married, to meet members of the opposite sex; or in certain cases to meet members of the same sex.
5. To have a cocktail and enjoy some particular local combo or band.
6. To get out of-the-house and enjoy a weekend Friday or Saturday night.
7. To celebrate with family and friends a special occasion, a birthday, an anniversary, a promotion, reunion, engagement, or farewell.
8. For the opposite reasons (to ease the pain following some sadness, such as a funeral.)
9. Just to stop by and check on the local scene; see if any of your friends are there.
10. Sometimes it is just a nice place to meet with friends to drink and chat.
11. Some large bars, i.e., Dave and Busters, ESPN, now offer so many forms of entertainment they have become an evening destination for bowling, television "watching," dancing, and games of chance.

232

12. To have a quick bite to eat, a slice of pizza, Buffalo wings, a burger, or to have a full dinner in a bar with a first class restaurant.

13. The bar with a drink is a wonderful place to appreciate life after a game of golf or softball, or tennis, or occasionally after just working around the house.

14. In many places, thankfully, the bar is still the poor man's country club where everyone knows your name. It's not just the booze; it's the bonding.

15. And there are the extravagant nightclubs that are there to help us enjoy top of the line entertainment and have a cocktail at the same time—Las Vegas, New York City, Miami, Chicago, casinos everywhere.

16. Enter your favorite reason or excuse.

With a list like this of occasions to visit a bar, and a record of serving the needs of human beings for over 2,000 years; it appears that the "watering hole" in some shape or form is safe for the future.

Here we are charging headlong into the 21st century and the bar continues to adapt to the needs of the people. We have mega sports bars with 80 TV screens, entertainment bars with hundreds and hundreds of games, swanky bars in casinos and night clubs—and we still have college hangouts, sleazy dumps, and thank God, neighborhood bars.

An old Irish phrase applies very well, "It's the same, but different."

SAMPLING OF FAMOUS BARS — WORTH A VISIT

The following is a short list and brief description of some of the historical bars and taverns still operating today.

NEW YORK CITY

St. Regis Hotel: The King Cole Room named after the mural by Maxfield Parish behind the bar. The secret (supposedly) is that an artist challenged Maxfield Parish to paint a fart. In any event, knowing that, it's entertaining to gaze at the mural. This room is also the birthplace of the Bloody Mary drink.

Waldorf-Astoria Hotel: The Bull and the Bear. A gathering spot for the rich and famous for over 100 years.

Algonquin Hotel: Oak Room Cabaret and the Blue Room, noted for Dorothy Parker's Round Table where famous writers of the day gathered to drink and exchange their wit. (West 44th Street near 6th Avenue.)

Carlyle Hotel: Café Carlyle and Bemelman's Bar, Ludwig Bemelman's murals—illustrator of the Madeline children's books. Frequented by the wealthy and famous.
(East 76th Street near Madison Avenue.)

White Horse Tavern: Built in 1880 and famous as the spot where Dylan Thomas proclaimed, "I've had eighteen straight whiskies, I think that's a record." He then died.
(567 Hudson Street at W. 11th Court, Greenwich Village.)

McSorley's: Opened in 1854. Lines down the block on Friday and Saturday evenings; still serve only light and dark ale. (15 Seventh Street, just off Cooper Square.)

Plaza Hotel: Oak Room Bar – Wonderful location in the Plaza Hotel where the rooms are $1,000 a night. The Oak Room Bar unusually establishes the upper limit for prices in New York City.

Bridge Café: Dates from 1794, originally a house of prostitution. Lower Manhattan.

P.J. Clarke's: Wonderful old New York bar. *Lost*

234

Weekend with Ray Millard was filmed here in 1945 (3rd Avenue at 55th Street).

Joe Allen's: On restaurant row, 46th Street between 8th and 9th Avenues. A before or after the theatre place. *All About Eve* was filmed here. Photos of the famous cover the walls.

Fraunces Tavern: A 1907 replica of the original 1717 building. A museum with an operating restaurant. (54 Pearl Street near Broad Street.)

Chumley's: This was a speakeasy during Prohibition, and it maintains its unmarked secret door and original ambience; with oak booths, fireplace and sawdust on the floor. For many years it was a literary hangout—Hemingway, John Steinbeck, Edna Ferber, Jack Kerouac, Simone Beauvoir, etc. (Greenwich Village, 86 Bedford near Barrow.)

Rainbow Room: Top of Radio City. What a view!!! Room closed; but bar is still open.

Stonewall Bar: Scene of the famous confrontation between New York police and gays. (53 Christopher Street) The original was next door at 51 Christopher.

21 Club: A famous speakeasy during Prohibition continues to draw crowds at lunch and dinner. (51st Street.)

Café des Artistes: History abounds in this 76-year-old establishment. Famous for murals of naked nymphs playing in a richly flowered forest.

SAN FRANCISCO:

Top of the Mark: Famous gathering spot for servicemen leaving for, or arriving from, the Pacific during World War II. Mark Hopkins Hotel

Pied Piper Bar: Located in the Palace Hotel and dates from 1875. Maxfield Parish mural behind the bar "The Pied Piper of Hamelin." Famous for "two olive martinis."

OAKLAND

Last Chance Saloon: This is the bar mentioned frequently in Jack London's books. In fact, London had a favorite table where he would often write. This place is small and dates from 1883. It is crowded with a plethora of stuff hanging from the walls and ceiling. Many of the furnishings are original, including the bar, gaslights and pot-bellied stove. (56 Jack London Square.)

BOSTON

Bull and Finch Pub: The original source for the hit TV Show of the '90s "Cheers." This bar was dismantled in England and shipped here. It does not resemble the bar scene on "Cheers." An exact replica of the Cheers bar has been re-created at another location.

Doyle's Café: A wonderful Irish Pub in an Irish City, dating from 1882. This place is a political landmark in a city noted for its politicians.

NEW ORLEANS

A city filled with wonderful bars that stay open all night. A town where you can stay in a bar all night; and at 7:00 A.M. greet an entirely new crowd just arriving. A town where you can stroll around carrying a drink.

Brennans: Try a real New Orleans specialty Sazerac,

made with Absinthe, simple syrup, Peychaud's bitters and a lemon twist. Bourbon or rye can substitute for Absinthe.

Antoines: Try a Ramos Fizz made with gin, cream, sugar, lemon juice, lime juice, club soda and an orange flower.

O'Briens: Famous, ironically, for the "Hurricane drink" made with rum and served in a 29 ounce hurricane lamp style glass.

Old Absinthe House: In its 200-year history guests have included Franklin Roosevelt, Mark Twain, Frank Sinatra and Oscar Wilde.

Napoleon House Bar and Grill: A must visit—one of the best bars in the United States.

Lafitte's Blacksmith Shop: Dating from 1770, it may be the oldest building in New Orleans. The pirates, Pierre and Jean Lafitte, used it as a "front" for disposing of their "ill-gotten" gains.

New Orleans is the home of the Museum of the American Cocktail. The place is filled with antique liquor bottles, Art Deco cocktail shakers, vintage swizzle sticks, Tiki cups, a library containing thousands of books about drinking, bartending, and drink recipes. The exhibit takes the visitor from the early 1800s through Prohibition, the Polynesian "Tiki" rage of the 1940s and '50s; to the "swinger" cocktail lounges of the 1960s and '70s.

FT. WORTH, TEXAS

Home of "Billie Bob's: Famous for being "big," even by the Texas standards; forty bars, indoor rodeo arena, two dance floors, live music every night, room for 6,000 people.

White Elephant Saloon: A true western saloon. Recalls the Olde West with a wooden stand-up bar, brass rail, etc. Gambler Luke Short outdrew and killed former Texas Marshall "Long Hair" Jim Court in the bar in 1887.

BUFFALO, NEW YORK

Frank and Teresa's Anchor Bar: Where spicy, hot, chicken wings were invented in 1964. The bar opened in 1935. The place is filled with memorabilia and photos of famous guests of the restaurant. The wings idea took place when friends came in late one evening after the kitchen had closed. Teresa Bellissimo, wife of the owner, took some chicken wings she had intended for soup stock, fried them, and tossed them with hot sauce she stirred up on the spot. They were an instant hit! They serve and ship over 2,000 pounds of chicken wings each day. Main Street.

Each year there is a Buffalo Wing Festival held at the baseball stadium that attracts over 40,000 people. The chicken wing eating contest record is 173 wings in 12 minutes, established in 2007.

CHICAGO

Billy Goat Tavern in the basement of the Wrigley building. This hole-in-the-wall has been a hangout for advertising and newspaper people forever. Michigan Avenue.

Signature Room and Bar: Located on the 96th floor of the John Hancock Building—wonderful views. Michigan Avenue.

Green Mill: Once owned by Al Capone. His photo is on the piano. Famous for jazz since 1907.

Omni Ambassador East Hotel: Pump Room. This place has played host to every visiting celebrity since the 1940s. All their photos decorate the wall. In its celebrity heyday Booth One was a special location. When Harry Carey was announcing the Chicago baseball games he stopped in every evening "to get ready."

Original Mother's: Around since the '60s and immortalized by Demi Moore, Jim Belushi and Rob Lowe in the film *About Last Night*. (26 Division Street.)

John Barleycorn: The building dates from 1890 and contains the original tin ceiling and two-feet thick walls. This was a Chinese laundry during the 1920s, and served as a "front" for bootleggers who rolled laundry carts of booze to the basement. John Dillinger was a frequent customer, often treating the house. The bar is filled with handmade replicas of ships collected by the former Dutch proprietor on his travels to the Far East. (658 W. Balden.)

ALEXANDRIA, VIRGINIA

Gadsby's Tavern Museum: Alexandria was the crossroads of 18th century America, and its social center was Gadsby's Tavern. The two buildings date from 1785 and 1792 respectively.

Innkeeper John Gadsby combined the two buildings to form "a gentlemen's tavern" which he opened in 1796. George Washington was a frequent guest, and celebrated his last birthday here. Other guests included Thomas Jefferson, James Madison and Lafayette. The tavern was the scene of lavish parties, theatrical performances, small circuses, government meetings, and concerts. Doctors and dentists treated their patients here. Fully restored with an operating restaurant and bar. (134 N. Royal Street.)

ROSLYN, WASHINGTON

The Brick: This tavern was used in the TV series Northern Exposure (1990-1995). The television show concerned life in a small town in Alaska; but it was actually filmed here. The Brick is the oldest operating pub in the state of Washington. The grand back bar is over 100 years old. Downtown Roslyn—1½ hours east of Seattle.

PHILADELPHIA

McGillin's Old Ale House: McGillin's is Philadelphia's oldest tavern, and the wall behind the bar is decorated with licenses dating to 1860, which somehow survived a devastating fire in 1971. A red tile floor dates to 1900, thick pillars support the beamed ceiling, and historic signs and pictures cover the walls. Long wooden tables fill the tavern, and a large stone fireplace dominates the back wall.

When Philadelphia's theater district was greater, this was a popular spot for actors who could slip through the back door. Will Rogers, John Barrymore, Tennessee Williams, Ethel Merman, Billy Daniels, and many more drank here.

City Tavern: Beginning in 1773 the original City Tavern served many a founding father. The current version is a faithful recreation of the original, capturing the colonial spirit and style. Corner of 2nd and Walnut Streets.

LOS ANGELES

Barney's Beanery: Founded in 1920 and famous for chili and its selection of over 70 beers. The place has been a celebrity hangout since its founding, over 80 years ago.

BALTIMORE

The Horse You Came In On: The legendary drinking hole of Edgar Allan Poe; who died an alcoholic. 1626 Thomas Street.

PRINCETON, NJ

Nassau Inn: Charming 1756 hotel features a Norman Rockwell mural and photographs of famous Princeton grads. Ten Palmer Square.

ACKNOWLEDGEMENTS

To all the delightful times spent with wonderful people in bars across this great Country.

I wish to acknowledge the support of my wife Babs during this long effort.

John O'Neill, Howard Kramer and Gere Coffey lent their support and offered valuable suggestions.

A special thank you to Neil Stalter for his encouragement and expert editing of the manuscript.

Ray Brush provided a wonderful final editing of the book

BIBLIOGRAPHY

Ade, George. *The Old-Time Saloon*. Old Town, 1993.

Barr, Andrew. *Drink: A Social History*. London: Pimlico, 1998.

Battenberry, Michael. *On the Town in New York*. Charles Scribner, 1973.

Behr, Edward. *Prohibition: Thirteen Years That Changed America*. Arcade
Publishing, 1996.

Blumenthal, Ralph. *Stork Club: America's Most Famous Nightspot and the
Lost World of Cafe Society*. Little, Brown and Co., 2000.

Brown, John Hull. *Early American Beverages*. C.E. Tuttle Co., 1966.

Colonial Williamsburg Foundation, Michael Olmert, and Suzanne E. Coffman.
Official Guide to Colonial Williamsburg. Colonial Williamsburg
Foundation, 1998.

Duis, Perry R. *The Saloon: Public Drinking in Chicago and Boston, 1880-
1920*. University of Illinois Press, 1998.

Earle, Alice. *Stagecoach and Tavern Days*. MacMillan, 1900.

Erdoes, Richard. *Saloons of the Old West*. Gramercy Books, 1979.

Erenberg, Lewis A. *Steppin' Out: New York Nightlife and the Transformation
of American Culture, 1890-1930*. University of Chicago Press, 1981.

Field, Edward. *The Colonial Tavern*. Providence, 1897.

Goodman, Jack. *While You Were Gone*. Simon and Schuster, 1946.

Kallen, Stuart A. *History Firsthand: The Roaring Twenties*. Greenhaven Press, 2001.

Klein, Jef. *The History and Stories of the Best Bars of New York*. Turner Publishing Co., 2006.

Larkin, Jack. *The Reshaping of Everyday Life, 1790-1840*. Harper and Rowe, 1988.

Lathrop, Elise. *Early American Inns and Taverns*. New York: Tudor Publishing Co., 1937.

London, Jack. *John Barleycorn*. Random House, 1913.

Malone, Audrey. *Historic Pubs of Dublin*. Prion Books Ltd, 2001.

Martin, Brian. *Tales from the Country Pub*. David & Charles Publishing, 1998.

Martin, Cy. *Whiskey and Wild Women*. Hart Publishing Co., 1974.

Martin, James and Lender, Mark. *Drinking in America*. New York: Free Press, 1982.

Mitchell, Joseph. *McSorley's Wonderful Saloon*. Pantheon Books, 1992.

Moehringer, J.R. *The Tender Bar: A Memoir*. Hyperion, Inc., 2005.

Modern Marvels: Saloons DVD. The History Channel. 2004.

Powers, Madelon. *Faces Along the Bar*. University of Chicago Press, 1998.

Rice, Kym S. *Early American Taverns for the Entertainment of Friends and Strangers*. Chicago: Regnery Gateway, 1983.

Rorabaugh, William. The *Alcoholic Republic: An American Tradition*. New York: Oxford University Press, 1979.

243

Salinger, Sharon. *Taverns and Drinking in Early America*. Johns Hopkins University Press, 2002.

Simmons, James. *Star Spangled Eden: 19th Century America Through the Eyes of Dickens, Wilde, Frances Trollope, Frank Harris and Other British Travelers*. Carrol & Graf Publishers, 2000.

Sylvester, Robert. *No Cover Charge: A Backward Look at the Night Clubs*. Dial Press, 1956.

The American Brew: History of Beer in America. Washington, D.C.: Here's to Beer, Inc., 2007.

Thompson, Peter. *Rum Punch and Revolution: Taverngoing and Public Life in Eighteenth-Century Philadelphia*. Philadelphia: University of Pennsylvania Press, 1999.

Tyrell, Ian. *Sobering Up: From Temperance to Prohibition in Antebellum America, 1800-1860*. Greenwood Press, 1979.

Walton, Stuart. *Out of It: A Cultural History of Intoxication*. Harmony Books, 2002.

Weiser, Kathy. *The Great American Bars and Saloons*. Chartwell Books, 2006.

West, Elliott. *The Saloon on the Rocky Mountain Mining Frontier*. University of Nebraska Press, 1979.